A FELT SENSE

A FELT SENSE

More Explorations of Psychoanalysis and Kabbalah

Michael Eigen

Routledge
Taylor & Francis Group

LONDON AND NEW YORK

First published in 2014 by Karnac Books Ltd.

Published 2018 by Routledge
2 Park Square, Milton Park, Abingdon, Oxon, OX14 4RN
711 Third Avenue, New York, NY 10017, USA

Routledge is an imprint of the Taylor & Francis Group, an informa business

British Library Cataloguing in Publication Data

A C.I.P. for this book is available from the British Library

  ISBN-13: 9781782201021 (pbk)

Edited, designed and produced by The Studio Publishing Services Ltd
www.publishingservicesuk.co.uk
e-mail: studio@publishingservicesuk.co.uk

CONTENTS

The word "sense" is one of those words that span and bring together many dimensions: sense on a sensory level, vital sensing, common sense, the sense of meaning in language, and other senses hard to pin down. It is linked with intuition and plays a role in relation to oneself and others in sensing what one is feeling. Besides the "five senses" there is proprioception and kinesthesia, elusive "feels" within the body. There is, too, what language names a "sixth sense", a "follow your nose" sense which blends with the scent of experience. How something tastes or smells on a psychological level. How our psyches, our personalities smell and taste.

*   *   *

Religious language helps bring out nuances of psychological states and psychology helps make the language of the spirit more meaningful to emotional concerns today. Each brings out possibilities of the other, since both grow from a common root: a root sense touching how it feels to be alive, the taste of life.

Michael Eigen

ABOUT THE AUTHOR

Michael Eigen worked with disturbed, especially psychotic, children in his twenties, then adults in his thirties onwards. He directed an institute program for working with creative individuals at the Center for Psychoanalytic Training and was the first Director of Educational Training at the Institute for Expressive Analysis. He was on the Board of Directors at the National Psychological Association for Psychoanalysis for eight years, first as Program Chair, then editor of *The Psychoanalytic Review*. He has taught at many institutes and colleges and gave talks and seminars internationally. In the past twenty years he taught and supervised mainly at the National Psychological Association for Psychoanalysis and the New York University Postdoctoral Program in Psychotherapy and Psychoanalysis. He gives a private seminar on Winnicott, Bion, Lacan and his own work, ongoing nearly forty years. *A Felt Sense: More Explorations on Psychoanalysis and Psychotherapy* is his twenty-second book. It is based on recent seminars given for The New York University Postdoctoral Contemplative Studies Project.

PREFACE

This book is an elaboration of my third and fourth seminars given for the New York University Postdoctoral Program in Psychotherapy and Psychoanalysis Contemplative Studies Project (April 2012 and November 2012). The first two were published in *Kabbalah and Psychoanalysis* (2012a). Many thanks to Dr James Ogilvie for inviting me to give these seminars, Jim Baumbach for putting them online, and Daniel Wentworth for transcribing them.

The present seminars begin with discussion of the distinction–union structure, which I take further than my previous writings (Eigen, 1986, 1993, 2011). I like to write *distinctionunion* without the link, indicating a structural process that permeates experience. It is a topic written about by many, an aspect of the "double" nature of experience. We live in different worlds or dimensions at the same time, experience difference and connection at the same time. The seminar explores this dimension in world spirituality, aspects of science, psychoanalysis, and clinical work. As it does so, numerous dual tendencies come into focus, such as surface–depth, space–time-infinity, materiality–immateriality, souls in Kabbalah, self-states in psychoanalysis, and intersection of capacities or tendencies in both.

The seminars unfold into intricate intertwining of processes depicted by psychoanalysis and Kabbalah, processes important in helping us live more richly. Religious language helps bring out nuances of psychological states and psychology helps make the language of the spirit more meaningful to emotional concerns today, spanning unspeakable depths to ins and outs of everyday experience. Each brings out possibilities of the other, since both grow from a common root: a root sense that is an underlying thread of this book.

In a recent paper (2013) I write,

> Winnicott, I feel, returns repeatedly to a 'root' sense of life, how it feels to be alive, the taste of life. His work is a series of attempts to give expression to the unfolding of this 'root' sense . . . Winnicott, in his way, had a sense, a gift, I suspect, that may not have been so fully realized without the psychoanalytic setting, as the latter grew in possibilities with his touch. (p. 121)

Bion (1994) uses the term "root" as a notation to suggest processes that branch off into various domains of feeling expressiveness: for example, poetry, religion, painting, music. We touch this in detail in Chapter Two, "The second seminar", as to how a felt sense grows, creating and following avenues of expression.

A "felt sense" works not only in the general culture, but also in psychotherapy or psychoanalysis. In elaborated form, one might ally it with intuition, perhaps an underpinning of intuition. It plays a role in relation to oneself and others in sensing what one is feeling. The word "sense" is one of those words that span and bring together many dimensions: sense on a sensory level, vital sensing, common sense, the sense of meaning in language, and other senses hard to pin down. Even on the level of textbook sensation, besides the "five senses" there is proprioception and kinaesthesia, elusive "feels" within the body, moving or still. Einstein said he thought with vague images and muscular feels, later translated into conceptual language. There are myriad variations.

There is, too, what language names a "sixth sense", or, again, "follow your nose"—where sense blends with the scent of experience. How something tastes or smells—and we mean this on a psychological level. How our psyches, our personalities smell and taste to ourselves and others.

Freud wrote of consciousness as a sense organ for psychical experience, sensing psychical states. In Kabbalah, to which Bion resonates, states stretch from everyday life to infinities of infinitesimal and infinite dimensions. As Bion's work unfolded, he became more concerned with intuiting infinities (Eigen, 1998, 2012a), part of the emotive substratum of what it feels like to be oneself with another in the room: a sense of self and other touching surface and depths, with a background of infinity, which, in practical terms, means stay open, more can happen—is happening.

The second seminar, especially, touches five souls of Kabbalah, which I relate to three dimensions I call (1) everyday me; (2) constant struggle; (3) Grace. Chapter One includes new details of work with an alcoholic patient. Chapter Two includes critical moments of helping a fearful but highly creative woman die. Aspects of psychosis, creativity, mysticism, and everyday life blend and have a say.

The main psychoanalytic heroes in this book are Bion and Winnicott. If you read *Kabbalah and Psychoanalysis* (2012a), you know Bion's remark, "I use the Kabbalah as a framework for psychoanalysis". This book expands on the intertwining of myth, dream, and everyday reality, which mark the prose and poetry of both. The main focus is psychic reality, with psychoanalysis and Kabbalah tools in this great enterprise of learning to work with ourselves.

Michael Eigen, PhD
New York City

CHAPTER ONE

The first seminar

A s is the custom of the NYU Contemplative Studies Project, we will begin with a short meditation, here a little guided meditation, a little quiet time in the beginning. I will speak some words. If you're inclined, let them run through you. Feel them, taste them.

[Spoken slowly, many pauses]

There is a great radiance in this room, a light lighter than light.

It pervades your body, all through you. It is your body.

Light beyond light. So bright it can't be seen.

An invisible light, your light.

Light everywhere.

* * *

There is a great darkness in this room.

Darkness darker than dark.

It pervades your soul. It is your soul.

A loving darkness.

A loving darkness that light can't dim.

You are darkness, darker than dark.

You are light, lighter than light.

Sit for some moments, held by the quiet of the dark and the glow of the light.

*   *   *

[During the guided meditation, someone came in late.]
It is fitting that we began with an interruption. Interruption is part of beginning. Interruptions are part of the path.

If there is one thing I am good at, it is saying the obvious. I have a love of the obvious. I have a hunch today, whatever we do, it will all be very obvious. When I was a child, I loved hearing the same stories over and over. As an adult, I love reading the same passages over and over. So, I am a friend of the obvious, a lover of the obvious.

I am going to start by doing some passages from the first chapter of *Contact with the Depths* (2011) on the distinction–union structure. But before doing that, I would like to read a little from the introduction about surface and depth. We do not necessarily say what depth is, but live from it, with it, speak from it. I ask in the introduction (p. xiii). "What of surface–depth connection? So many possibilities of connection–disconnection. We are sensitive to new structures, emergence of capacities, discontinuity, evolution, gaps between dimensions, splits between affective attitudes, divisions. Yet, there is also a fit between surface–depth."

In postmodern times, we are used to emphasising rupture, disconnection, lacunae, gaps, but there is also a fit between surface and depth. "A moment of beauty makes us quiver through and through, reverberates through our being, touches foundations, an experience that ripples through sensation, feeling, thinking, action, ethics" (p. xiii). A moment of beauty runs through it. In the very centre of the *Sephirot*, the Kabbalah tree of life (Figure 1), the very centre, the heart of the *Sephirot*, is *Tiferet*, usually translated as beauty.

Beauty ripples through us. As Keats says, a thing of beauty is a joy forever. "At that moment, the gap is bridged, suspended (not

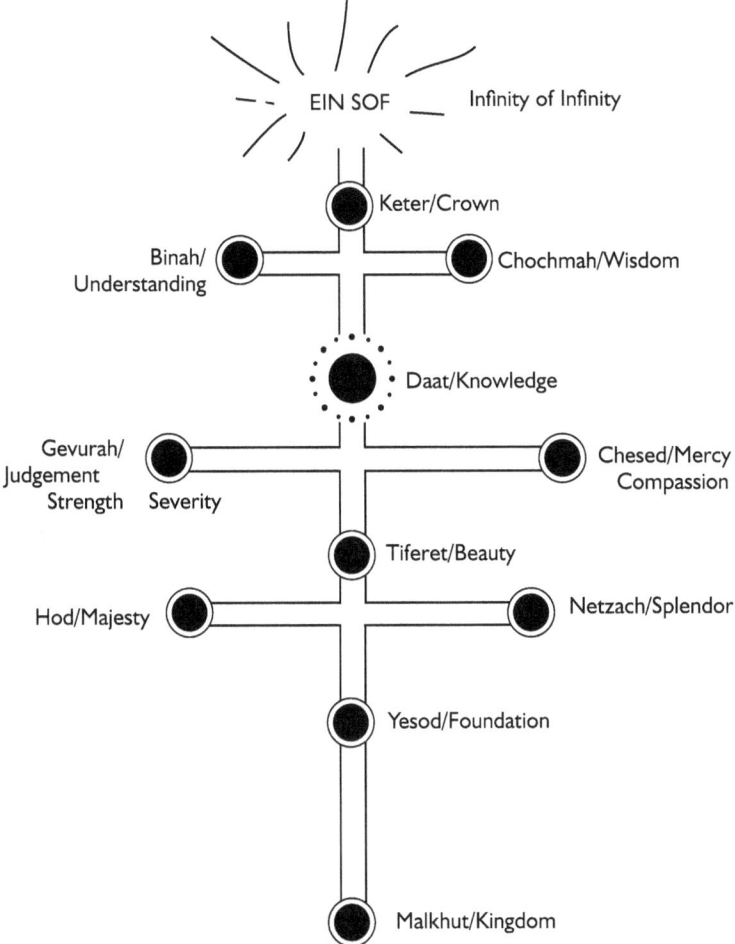

Figure 1. *Ein Sof* and the *Sephirot* (Tree of Life).

obliterated). Connection between outside–inside and inner layering permeates us and we realise how interlaced we are with what, at other times, might seem remote. Consciousness not only separates, it brings together, it turns possibilities around, interlocks, fuses" (p. xiii). Tendencies to distinguish and unite work together. Think of metaphor: in metaphor you have distinct elements and an unexpected link is made between them, perhaps a mixture of resonance and disjunction. Something new comes into being and for a time you cannot tell the difference between distinction and union. It just happens. A structure that both distinguishes and unifies, a union–distinction structure with double aspects, a double or multiple structure involving sub-structural processes. Sometimes we describe this as a "flash" or insight, perception of new relations and connections, vision of the "whole" (temporary whole), not quite seen before, not quite that way.

Interfusion of surface and depth characterises growth of sensitivity. Similarly, interfusion of word-wordlessness. A deep sense of unknowing often provides a background linking presence in daily life. We are creatures of diverse and paradoxical capacities. We need to make and break connections, start again, undo and redo, as if what we create makes us claustrophobic.

At the end of the introduction, I write, "Our mixed capacities can stymie us, cause confusion, a kind of centipede not knowing how to use its legs. But they also are a source of plasticity, ability to survive, and survive well if only we keep on learning how to use our evolving makeup, do not give up on it, or it on us."

In the beginning of the book, I have a few sayings. The first two I wrote: "Whatever happens opens reality". Of course, that cannot be true—or can it? The other saying is, "One never recovers from being human". There are two more sayings, one by Dogen: "Its exquisite peel permeates everywhere"; one by Merle Molofsky: ". . . of trust and trembling fears, a spark, as in the beginning".

*   *   *

Now I would like to speak more about distinction–union and say the obvious. We make distinctions and connect. One way Freud expresses this is by positing dual tendencies, a life drive that creates unities and a death drive that unties, breaks, or falls apart, integrating–disintegrating, building–destroying. I say "break or falls apart" because there seem to be different ways of talking about death drive, one a more active process of breaking apart, the other a more passive falling apart, collapsing, entropy. For Freud, libido is active. He depicts an active psyche even in passivity. Passivity is not usually passive for Freud. Yet, there does seem to be a passive dropping away connected with the death drive, as when character wears itself out by its lifelong conflicts and gives way.

Many depth psychologists have their own ways of expressing this double tendency, individuation–union, separation–symbiosis, towards dependency–towards independence, splitting–fusion, disjunction–conjunction, symmetry–asymmetry— you may have your favourites. An ancient set of capacities, but we might not be aware that they are always working together in varied ways. They can be dissociated, antagonistic, symbiotic, oppositional, mutually self-destructive, but they also can be co-nourishing, indistinguishable.

Sometimes I depict distinction–union as branches of a single trunk or parts of complex root systems. Freud, Winnicott, and Bion speak about indistinguishable origins of psychic tendencies. Our cognitive capacities often make binaries of what begins together and remains intermixed. We often speak of complementary and oppositional dynamics of discriminated differences.

Bion speaks of unobservable transformations and sometimes uses the notation T in O to signal unknown, unobserved transformational processes, O a notation for unknown, perhaps unknowable reality— in psychoanalysis, emotional reality. Buddhism also speaks of nameless Buddha lands suggestive of rapid transformational work outside awareness. This takes us to a place that is something other or more than making the unconscious conscious. Much depends here on quality of unconscious functioning, unconscious work. Bion speaks of making the conscious unconscious. By this he means making something part of us, letting life in, letting our own life in. Letting our own life seep deep into our unknown, unconscious substructures that support conscious living. The quality of the one influences the quality of the other.

The Holy Trinity is a good cultural example of difference-in-union. As the experience/concept began to be formulated there were doctrinal disagreements. Are these three substances? Three Persons? The Council of Nicaea in 325 CE decided it was one substance yet three Persons, the Father, Son, and Holy Spirit. One-yet-three, three yet truly One. A union of indistinguishable–distinguishable. A mystery.

Similarly, the *sh'ma Yisrael*, which often is translated, "Hear O Israel, the Lord is God, the Lord is One". *Sh'ma Yisrael, Adonai Elohenu, Adonai echad. Sh'ma*—hear. *Yisrael*—Israel. *Adonai*—Lord is substituted orally for the written Tetragramaton, *YHVH*, a central name of God throughout much of Torah. As tradition developed, it became Unsayable, connoting God beyond conception, images, language. *Adonai*—Lord, is said in its place.

Elohenu is also a word for God—plural, gods. YHVH (*"Yahveh"*—singular, the One, God of God). *Elohenu*—plural. *Echad*—One. The One is the many, the many the One. Singular–plural, distinguishable–indistinguishable, distinction–union. A mystical sense of the Allness–Oneness of the God beyond representational capacity (Eigen, 2012a).

In the *Bhagvad Gita*, everything is Krishna. Arjuna, a warrior, argues with Krishna. Arjuna does not want to kill, especially those close to him. There appears to be a difference between the One and the many, but Krishna prevails, unleashing an awesome vision of his Oneness in Everything, including a forceful sense that Krishna is Arjuna as well. Difference gives way and Arjuna will do what he has to. Perhaps, as time goes by, this could reveal a conflict in Krishna between competing tendencies (war and peace), a conflict within the human psyche, as yet not resolved.

The one and the many is an ancient sensation taking different forms. In Saint Paul we are one body in Christ, yet many beings. You are just you. No one can be you but you—and yet . . .

David Bohm (1996), a physicist, distinguishes between explicate–implicate orders. In the implicate dimension, everything is connected with everything else, parts of unknown transformational processes. The explicate order has to do with individual distinctions, consciousness of this in contrast with that. They are two modes of being, double-in-one capacities: you are me and I am you; you are not me and I am not you. What we see, hear, think are handles of the pot, levers we grab on to and utilise. We can turn light switches on and off but do not now how the electricity really works. We are expressions of little known or unknown processes at work throughout the universe. Part of the feeling of creativeness we participate in reflects a sense of processes creating us, including a generative sense of self and other coming into being.

The psychoanalyst Matte-Blanco (1988) wrote of symmetrical and asymmetrical modes of being. In the former, all members of a set share a common identity. For example, the class of mothers: all mothers are women. By symmetrical reversal, the psyche yields identity spread: all women are mothers. In the asymmetrical mode, individual women maintain their individual differences, mothers or not. The symmetrical mode is given to psychic contagion and union, the asymmetrical mode to distinction. Sometimes I call the former *oneness experiencing/thinking*, the latter two-ness, three-ness, multi-individual, *difference experiencing/thinking*. Matte-Blanco feels both tendencies are part of every psychic act.

Bion (1994a, p. 169) writes of a woman deathly afraid of the urge to exist. She is deathly afraid of the urge to exist because it could kill her. She is thinking of the urge to be a mother but fears that becoming a mother will kill her. There is conflict between the individual and what Freud called the racial instinct, the drive to procreate or do what is necessary in order to perpetuate the human species, whether or not *you* want to. A tension between collective forces and a particular individual, between what is "good" for the collective and what is "good" for the individual. A social example: the group telling me to go to war when *I* do not want to go to war. My body does not want to go to war or, the woman Bion speaks of, I do not want to have a baby. Tension between individual and larger forces of existence that push one or, at least, exert enormous pressure.

There are many variations and tangles. For example, I may fight larger forces in order to preserve myself, yet lose out on fuller development because of the energy involved in fighting. I might become paranoid about my own nature, fighting myself in order to save myself, yet remain stunted in order to stay alive. In Matte-Blanco's terms, there is asymmetrical me. Little me and you, very valuable to me and you, *vs.* symmetrical being pushing us towards self-destruction because of a "greater" cause. Bion's patient remains shut in on herself to preserve herself. Bion notes the urge to exist does not care whether an individual lives or dies—as long as existence continues. He writes from experience. His first wife died in childbirth and, unknown to him, the child of that birth was to perish in a car accident in the Italian mountains a few years after she helped organise a meeting honouring the centenary of her father's birth. We experience ourselves and live our lives in both creative and destructive keys. What does one do when one experiences one's urge to exist as destructive? So much more complicated because symmetrical experience can be ecstatic, whether in destructive or life-giving mode. To feel *one-with* can go many ways.

Bion speaks of faith in face of destructive tendencies and calls faith the psychoanalytic attitude, which he sometimes describes as being without memory, desire, understanding, and expectation. Faith in the moment itself. Or faith in face of the moment. His notation for this:

F in O. Faith in face of unknown psychic forces that can destroy you and/or give rise to what might be felt as catastrophic change. A psychoanalytic analogue to the mystic's darkness that begets faith more brightly, a profoundly lived paradox.

F in O, T in O. Faith and transformation linked with psychical depths that defy usual kinds of representation. Coming through is sometimes expressed as a sense of at-oneness. A sense that opens realities one did not know possible.

In part, I think of Dogen's (Tanahashi, 1995, pp. 76–83) portrayal of flowing time, present flowing into future, present flowing into past, past into present, present flowing into present, future into future—transformations of *threeone*. I am purposely writing three and one as *threeone* to convey a sense of reality working. In a lifetime, and in psychoanalysis, what we think of as past or present or future changes radically the more we open to time moments. Yesterday, today, tomorrow change each other as we wade more fully into our lived time field. As we peel off dead skin, all time comes alive. Or, as Dogen might say, this moment is all moments. Aspects of time: distinguishable–indistinguishable.

Let me ask what is probably an unfair question. In the *Zohar*, in the Kabbalah, what is the biggest tree in the garden? (No hands, pause.) The biggest tree in the garden is the Tree of Faith. The tree of knowledge (K) is a smaller tree, even if it gets us into a lot of trouble. Knowledge is power, so no underestimating it. Give the power and ecstasy of knowledge its due, so often it lights our lives as well as torments us. Perhaps in another seminar we can spend more time relating these two "trees", K and F. Faith, in this context, is associated with life, the Tree of Life. We speak of faith in life or the role faith plays in life. We speak of disillusionment. So much therapy involves a crisis of faith in face of disillusionment. The Tree of Faith is the Tree of Life, the heart of the garden, connected with Tiferet, beauty that touches life. If we went into this, we would be led into discussion of what ways faith and life do and don't go together, intertwining yes–no.

In "The area of faith in Winnicott, Lacan and Bion" (1981, 2004), I traced relationships between faith and knowledge. It would be interesting to bring together Bion's grid (Figure 2) and O-grams (Figures 3 and 4), the Kabbalah *Sephirot*, or Tree of Life (see Figure 1. p. 3), and Kundalini *chakras*. Their differences and interplays open fruitful possibilities of experiencing. Perhaps we will try to do this in another

THE GRID

	Definitory Hypotheses	ψ	Notation	Attention	Inquiry	Action	
	1	**2**	**3**	**4**	**5**	**6**	**. . . n**
A β-elements	**A1**	**A2**				**A6**	
B α-elements	**B1**	**B2**	**B3**	**B4**	**B5**	**B6**	**. . . Bn**
C Dream Thoughts Dreams, Myths	**C1**	**C2**	**C3**	**C4**	**C5**	**C6**	**. . . Cn**
D Pre-conception	**D1**	**D2**	**D3**	**D4**	**D5**	**D6**	**. . . Dn**
E Conception	**E1**	**E2**	**E3**	**E4**	**E5**	**E6**	**. . . En**
F Concept	**F1**	**F2**	**F3**	**F4**	**F5**	**F6**	**. . . Fn**
G Scientific Deductive system		**G2**					
H Algebraic Calculus							

Figure 2.   Bion's Grid.

seminar. There is relevant material in the Appendices of *Kabbalah and Psychoanalysis* (2012a). Merle Molofsky (2009) has a paper online in which she talks about Qi Gong and the *Sephirot* and the *chakras* ("Some thoughts on synthesizing concepts in the *chakra* system, Jewish mystical tradition and Qi Gong", 2009). She envisions Jacob's ladder as the seven *chakras*. There is so much to touch and be touched by.

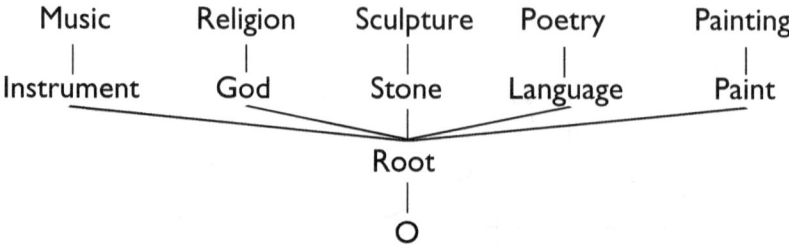

Figure 3. O-gram 1 (Bion, 1994b, p. 323).

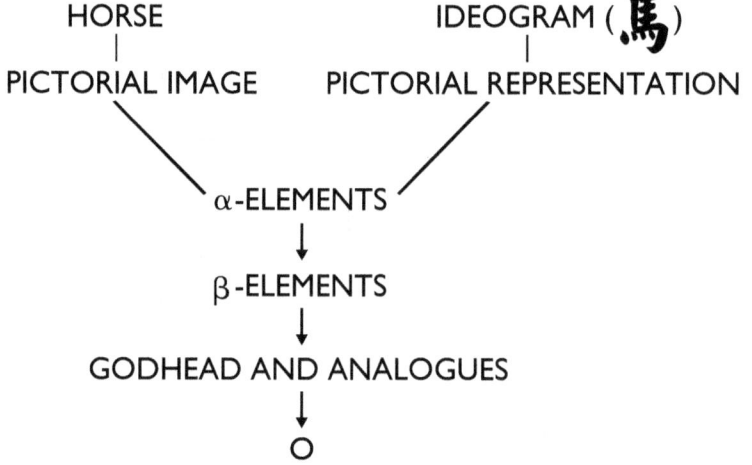

Figure 4. O-gram 2 (Bion, 1994, p. 325).

For both Matte-Blanco and Bion, infinity is a basic part of their writing as it unfolds. In *The Unconscious as Infinite Sets* (1975), Matte-Blanco associates infinity with unconscious life. There are many levels and qualities of unconscious infinites. He says, in relation to psycho-analysis, "Infinity is here to stay".

Bion (1994b, p. 372) writes, "The fundamental reality is 'infinity', the unknown, the situation for which there is no language—not even one borrowed by the artist or the religious—which gets anywhere near to describing it."

We may not "know" O but we can live it, work with it as it lives us. Knowledge plays a role as well. I think of Buddha exercised by the fact of suffering, sitting with the fact of suffering. Sitting with the pain of life, staying with it, staying with it until something happens. The psyche perforates, a kind of wormhole, and you find yourself somewhere else. In Buddha's case, Nirvana. How does that happen? Start here, find yourself there. You sit with an unsolvable problem, banging your head against a wall, then find yourself somewhere else. Samsara–Nirvana, distinction–union throughout both: are there states beyond both?

Bion posits a destructive force that goes on working after it destroys everything. It feeds on destruction. It never stops destroying, it cannot do anything else. He posits Faith as the only attitude that can meet such a force. Perhaps faith after all faith has been destroyed. Is it possible that faith replenishes itself, is ever in process of being born even as it is being destroyed? I think of Job: Yea though You slay me, yet will I trust You.

We are touching something that can happen, soul happening, soul-work. In a particular individual, there is no predicting the outcome.

At the end of *A Memoir of the Future* (1990), Bion writes,

> All my life I have been imprisoned, frustrated, dogged by common-sense, reason, memories, desires and—greatest bug-bear of all—understanding and being understood. This is an attempt to express my rebellion, to say 'Good-by' to all that. It is my wish, I now realize doomed to failure, to write a book unspoiled by the tincture of common-sense, reason, etc. (see above). So although I would write, 'Abandon Hope all ye who expect to find any facts—scientific, aesthetic or religious—in this book', I cannot claim to have succeeded. All these will, I fear, be seen to have left their traces, vestiges, ghosts hidden within these words; even sanity, like 'cheerfulness', will creep in. However successful my attempt, there will always be the risk that the book 'became' acceptable, respectable, honoured and unread. 'Why write then?' you may ask. To prevent someone who KNOWS from filling the empty space—but I fear I am being 'reasonable', that great Ape. Wishing you all a Happy Lunacy and a Relativistic Fission . . . (p. 578)

I love the mixture of humour, irony, love, frustration: affirmation as tendencies cross wires, act as barriers and nourishment. Explosive fusion, happy madness, thought that cannot be stopped. What is he after in writing this book? To write beyond writing? To write beyond words, beyond The Word? In a way, limits of our equipment frustrate us. There is a longing to get beyond everything we can think and feel, to touch Home Base, the Other, the mystery of mysteries. To get beyond the veil of all we can construct, all personality barriers. We feel hemmed in by our means of communication and contact, our avenue of access. Moments of freedom, moments of hell, loss, imponderable walls, no access. Yet, in the beginning of *Cogitations* (1994b) Bion—or is it his editor, Francesca Bion, as *Cogitations* was published posthumously—quotes Poincaré: "Thought is only a flash between two long nights, but this flash is everything".

Unknown, unseen Transformations in O—dimly intimated, through a glass darkly, shadows on a wall. It is said that Bodhidharma meditated in front of a wall for nine years. What wall was he facing? Milner (1987) calls Bion's O zero (0). A lot goes on in zero land. One waits in zero, trembles over zero, hovers within zero; one and zero hovering over and within each other. Creative waiting. Winnicott and Bion repeatedly write of premature closing off of O-work, often by K. K can mediate O and O transmit in K, but, too often, there is impatience, "irritable reaching after facts and reasons", conclusions, closing the hole in the circle.

Picture a break in the line around the circle, the line that makes the oval or circle, the line that makes the O or 0. Even on the level of perception we might not notice the break, the opening. Our eyes–brain might complete the line. Is it not part of therapy to help build tolerance for incompletion? Part of the work is to see into ways we tried to fill in, complete what cannot be completed, or must be left open. Always doubleness, multiplicity in this work, building tolerance for better ways of feeling "whole", partly based on better ways of tolerating "no-whole". Eddington on the universe: something unknown is doing we do not know what. We are part of the unknown, or, some might say, the unknown responding to itself. Tingling with knowledge and know-how, supported by infinite darkness.

Distinctionunion—often these tendencies work in unconscious ways. I think of a case early in my practice many of you have heard about before. He first appeared in my writings in 1973 in a paper, "Abstinence and the schizoid ego", collected in *The Electrified Tightrope* (1993). Although these tendencies work invisibly, they also can become semi-visible. We will call this patient, as I did forty years ago, Abe. In case you have the delusion that you forget patients—you do not forget. All your sins haunt you and some good things come back to you, too. Why do I keep speaking about Abe? Hoping each time to go a little further, find a little more? Open a door that cannot be seen? A little different with each telling?

Abe was an alcoholic, as was his father. Unlike his father, he sought help. He would find himself lying in the street after a binge, without awareness of the passage of time. Frequently, he would come to himself and days had passed him by. Perhaps there was some succour in drunken stupor. A way of getting to that mystical darkness, peace beyond all that hems one in. Well, I am jumping ahead of myself.

He was in Alcoholics Anonymous, with much benefit, but it was the combination of therapy and AA that did the trick. He would intermittently stay dry, then binge. When things were good, people in his life were happy. When things were bad, everyone was worried and sad. It was very like a Greek chorus formed around his state. I somehow semi-consciously sensed this up–down as part of a pattern, a unity of a kind, an experiential arc. Although I could feel happier when he was all right and lower when he was low, I realised we were on a habitual rollercoaster together.

There was another part of me, also a spontaneous part of my nature, perhaps enhanced by training. Some still, steadfast aspect of consciousness that was more outside the storm, quietly being with life as it ticked its way through chronic upheavals. It was not a quiet Abe was used to. His father was prone to drunken rages in which, at times, he would piss on the living-room floor. His mother was helplessly critical, doing what she could when she could, but mostly doing what she could to get out of the way. Therapy was different. It stayed in the still point of the centre, for better or worse.

In time, Abe began to withdraw. He stayed at home, holing up most of the time. He seemed to lose interest in AA, in work, in his girlfriend, in his life. He became silent in sessions, as if something sucked him down. I was worried. Was what I thought the peace of his sessions a schizoid element in my personality that was creating a vacuum? Was I provoking a suicide? Here I was, a youngish therapist starting practice—would it all get derailed because of my lack, incapacity, incompetence? It brought me to the edge of ability. I didn't know what helped or what did not. Another possibility: we would both be homeless.

Then an act of grace. About eight months into his growing isolation, Abe came in and reported an amazing experience. He saw and felt a radiant I-point. He could not quite locate it: around his eyes, in his chest, through him, above him? His I aglow. An indestructible I-kernel radiating. Some fear but mostly thrilling peace. Within a few months, the radiance expanded to include nature, people—the world aglow. Outside–inside, inside–outside—glowing. Binging stopped. He went back to AA and his girlfriend moved in with him. Our therapy continued several years more and his gains continued.

What happened? Could this light be reached without profound aloneness? Without the therapy background to support this aloneness in hidden ways? A paradoxical combination, alone yet not alone, not alone yet alone. Distinctionunion of a kind. But more. What is this more? In *Flames From the Unconscious* (2009), I amplify Winnicott's writings about the mother as a background presence supporting the baby's aloneness. Winnicott (1988) writes of a dependence the baby does not know it has. A kind of infinite unknown background that supports existence in a relatively seamless way, perhaps akin to Balint's (1967) interpenetrating harmonious mix-up, or inter-permeating. In Abe's case, background support was wounded; consequently, deep quiet aloneness was wounded. Drunken stupor seemed a way of getting there, a way of tasting it, mimicking it. Profound blackouts, moments of peace at a destructive price.

Now, I do not want to paint myself as bringer of peace. I have my own serious problems. Abe probably could sense variable moods and areas of my personality, a number of "self systems" working, up–down, stormy–clear, loony–serious, closed–open, fatigued–ready. But also something even, not exactly unflappable and unbudging, but kind of an even keel. I think of Bion's description of keeping a clear head in battle, or Freud's eye in the storm. Something that just goes on, through wave after wave. I used to call it a steel-trapped mind but it is not steel, although maybe trapped. The part that could see Abe's climb and slide as a single movement rather than split, sense a difference between the light switch and the electricity, intimations of O-transformations in O-land.

The human race for so long seems trapped in opposites and categories. Our social thinking (and experiencing) splits into groupings, race, gender, money, power, talent, higher–lower. The Bible ends with Moses asking if we will choose good or evil. Freud ends wondering if we will choose life or death? Jewish mysticism, similarly, asks if you will be a *tzadik* or *rasha*, righteous, wise, or bad. There are extreme realities. But is anyone not a mixture? So much pressure to be one or the other, right or wrong, true or false. So much pressure from ideals and extremes, not to mention envious perception of inequities along personal or social scales.

And what of the life drive? Is it so good? Ambition, lust, hunger for food and power, desire for—fill in the blank. The first word in the Western canon, Homer's *Iliad*, is "Rage", consequent upon erotic theft. All within the circumference of Life. War because of the life drive, possession, desire. The ancient Greeks knew Eros meant trouble as well as bliss, Cupid with his arrows, often in the service of revenge. Always pressure to choose between unviable alternatives. The control model has done some good things, but also throws us off the scent. To be in control—control of what? Who or what is in control of what? What we mostly learn is we do not know what we are doing when it comes to working with ourselves. Who we are and what to do with it is up for grabs. How do we become partners with capacities that constitute us? What would a partnership model look like across many dimensions?

Who was in control of the process that unfolded with Abe? What happened seemed to have a life of its own. At best, we gave it chance to work. Perhaps the attitude I am groping for has something to do with transcendence? A little bit of transcendent vision goes a long way. Maybe what I called waiting has something to do with transcendence. Waiting on the unknown, involving implicit faith that something more might happen, something good, good enough, something worth waiting for. Maybe transcendent is the wrong word. Maybe subtendent would be better, if one can coin a term for the underneath creative possibility. Mute, unconscious body-English one tries to partner, that sometimes enables, sometimes blocks. Can one know what one will give birth to?

Einstein spoke of thinking–sensing in vague body sensations and images, later translated into higher order formulations. I do not know if there are any Einsteins in psychoanalysis or if there can be. But our work is not without "genius", a kind of psychoanalytic sensing, mostly unconscious, semi-conscious. Unconscious work we best not trust or mistrust, but somehow get the knack of mediating, glimpsing, through a lifelong process. As Socrates said of himself, something of midwife and gadfly. Socrates claimed to know more than others because he knew he was ignorant. A kind of knowing ignorance. I think psychoanalytic knowing or not-knowing has an element of humble waiting. Waiting in the dark. A waiting faith with nothing but faith to "hold on to"—psychoanalytic faith. Sensing. Mute sensing.

Perhaps terms like transcending–subtending are off. Maybe Bion's emphasis on binocular vision is closer. Seeing things with different psychic eyes, each with different messages about reality, creative acts arising between them.

Winnicott (1988, p. 76) drew a diagram suggesting that inner bad objects outnumber inner good objects, but the little good goes a long way. So, a little bit of transcendent–subtendent or binocular work goes a long way, sometimes making a difference between suicide and living. In my imagination, I see a baby tossed to and fro, heights of joy one moment, depths of agony the next. Health providers can make this link with babyhood and sense acute affect dramas one goes through. This affect sense happens automatically, partly a result of training, but also partly a gift, a talent. Perhaps a significant portion of individuals who go into our field are the kind of people who have affect vision, a sensibility for baby life. This might be so even if they are dissociated from what they sense. The sensing is there. One hopes that it develops with use over time; a sense aching to be used. Perhaps this is a basis for gratitude to patients, providing opportunity to use capacities that need to develop.

I suspect awareness of infant affect dramas is more radical now than in most eras of human history. Grown men as well as women study what babies go through, professions of learning about babies. I first saw Beatrice Beebe's slow motion films, micro-moments of mother–infant interaction when she was Daniel Stern's research assistant. The films she produced then, and over an important career since, are consciousness raising, documenting moment to moment, back and forth affect flow. I do not think that flow ever stops, although, as adults, we learn to play it down and make believe it is not there, unless it becomes unmanageable. Technology, sensibility, and interest make films like Beebe's possible, something new for the human race.

For the moment, I want to posit that each state lasts forever. And, as adults, we have our forever moments. Once time consciousness develops more fully, there are states of hell we would like to see end quickly and heavenly states we wish would go on. In my imaginings of baby states that go on forever, there is a still point of awareness, a witness or seer, one who goes on noticing in the midst of emotional storms, even in the depths of madness. A seer present to Abe's upheavals and my fears and incapacity. In this case, a seer who could do little but wait. It has taken many years to learn about and cultivate creative waiting, although I sensed it in nascent form near the beginning.

It did not take too long for me to realise Abe was withdrawing from social life. It took longer to see he also was withdrawing from alcohol. To see the whole arc of this experience, contraction–expansion, took time. It paralleled in a positive way what his climbs up, spins down did in a more destructive mode. Both were attempts at communication, showing an x that was wrong. But the new happening, contraction–expansion, discovering radiance, was healing.

Khan (1996) was one of the few analysts who wrote about creative silence in patients. Most workers at the time usually interpreted silence as resistance rather than potentially healing. There are many kinds of silence and, like getting used to "seeing in the dark", one gradually develops a silence sense that discriminates silence from silence. Milner and Winnicott also had this "feel". A certain quiet is needed for processing of feelings. I remember a good practitioner talking about dreams as resistance. Silence, dreams, anything could be interpreted as resistance. Resistance to what? The practitioner I am thinking of said resistance to interpersonal connection. Well, there is a psychoanalytic kaleidoscope, and any way you turn it there is truth, up to a point.

Khan also linked a positive silence to a deeper sense of surrender, which, at times, talk defends against. Is psychoanalysis saying anything can be a defence against anything else? So much depends on a sense of nuance and how one interprets it. Sometimes I think we all dip into the same water, but have different explanations. In Abe's case, I can vouch for the emergence of creative stillness linked with profound healing possibilities. Unexpected contact with an ineffable, mysterious, pulsating point, that he identified as his I, which soon expanded to include all I's.

Although location of this I-radiance cannot be pinned down, it includes something of an eye–heart glow—links between the sixth and fourth *chakras* (third eye and heart *chakras*) and between *Sephirot* 1-2, 6 (*Chochma-Binah* and *Tiferet*; Figure 1, p. 3). A glow that spreads, a caring centre everywhere, as if tasting an indestructible I-kernel made generosity possible.

I am not presenting this as a model for mystical experience or the enlightenment journey. Just one man's experience that I was partner to. Mystical experience takes many forms (Eigen, 1998) and even among the enlightened there are warring schools. No alpha–omega here, just one man's healing happening. The testimony is in the fruits, no more binging and the growth of more life.

Patients like Abe helped me to open up. But it is also true that something in me needed this opening and was asking for it without awareness. Psychoanalysis spans many levels. It might not be necessary or possible to touch all of them. To an important extent, one goes where the patient goes and finds worlds enough to work with. We are inherently permeable beings and affect each other on many levels, some with more awareness than others, some without any discernible conscious awareness at all, at least not what we usually mean by conscious. Freud was tempted to speak of unconscious work as unconscious consciousness, but even that is too confining to do it justice.

Inherent permeability makes us subject to influence, including transmission of feeling. Over time, such transmission can tip the balance for better or worse. Our inherent permeability forms the background of our work. Personality and identity are the foreground, a kind of funnel for background permeability. I am a quieter person than Abe was used to, given his stormy background. Quieter yet present, with resources that Abe sensed. We felt our way into the darkness and the darkness took over. And Abe is still alive today, living a decent life, and I am still practising.

Invisible good feelings in the background of our beings. Bad as I was, I was generally a milder traumatic presence than his parents and perhaps a milder traumatic presence than he was to himself. I tried not to piss on the floor too much. The spirit of the moment gets transmitted in little things as well. "How are you?" "I feel crummy." "Did you see the Knicks game?" "It's cold outside. Thank goodness it's warm enough here." Good enough feeling absorbed over long enough time.

When I was younger, I used to joke, "Thank God for psychoanalysis, it keeps me off the streets." In our own ways, Abe and I were supportive presences for each other, whatever else was in the mix. My patients gave me something to organise my life around, otherwise who knows what would have happened to me. On another plane, I think of someone like Winnicott, for whom the psychoanalytic setting enabled fuller use and development of his special creativity. Would he have been Winnicott without his patients?

Winnicott (1988) depicts variations in the emotional surround, variable vibratory effects of changing emotional weather. Moment to moment shifts in the surrounding emotional field make waves that spread through the infant's being. The way life feels shifts spontaneously, like instant to instant shifts in barometric pressure. So-called outside and inside worlds permeate and resist each other, informing aspects of unconscious life that supports and overturns. Buffeted by intermittent waves, we might not know why or how things happen or what they are. We do our best to ride them out, often going under, disappearing. Disappearing for a time that might seem eternal. The emotional seas that move through our beings blend into a vast unit that forms the background of our beings, the background of our lives.

In Abe's case, inherent permeability and unconscious background emotional support were wounded. He was wounded as personality began to form and continued forming. In his essay, "Psychology of madness" (Winnicott, 1992; Eigen, 2004, 2009) writes about trauma hitting as personality begins to form. An inference I draw from his work is that with such a background, one might be ever fearful of beginnings, plagued by fear of disaster associated with beginnings. One fears beginning will trigger a traumatic hit. You can see something like this working in Abe's pattern of good moments followed by bad, sobriety followed by binging. Beginning something good triggered something bad, a kind of ever-aborted experiential arc. In contrast, therapy supported a situation in which Abe's psyche, in conjunction with mine, created a sequence wherein beginnings were sustained and led to something creative. Growth of sustaining capacity is itself creative.

One of the most creative moments was emergence of I-radiance, which expanded to encompass everything, radiance that uplifts existence. Its spontaneous occurrence is akin to the wormhole I talked about in connection with Buddha (above, p. 10). Extreme contraction followed by expansion, starting one place, finding oneself in another. The story of Job also has this form. Extreme contraction, everything stripped away, followed by mystic revelation of an Awesome Power, after which life expanded once more. Intensity perforates the psyche and you find yourself somewhere else. One of my favourite Hebrew names for God is *Hamakom*, which means "the place", God as The Place. A Place that takes us to new places a moment before unheard of.

The Seder at Passover follows a similar structure: (1) contraction—slaves in Egypt, in Hebrew called *mitzrayim*, connoting a narrow place, narrow strait, narrow limit, (2) intensity of agony rises until a fathomless cry bursts forth which God hears, initiating movement towards (3) the vicissitudes of greater freedom. A basic rhythm, a rhythm of faith: closed–open, coming through. New life begins and new vicissitudes, a rhythm that takes many forms all life long. A rhythm which therapy with Abe unconsciously sustained.

Life is a blend of birth and aborted birth, often with startling variations. The birth story portrayed in the Seder, for example, is still in progress, outcome still at stake. Excruciating birth, promise of birth, aborted birth, moment after moment. Kafka calls our whole life an incomplete moment, an incomplete ongoing birth. Are we ever fully born? Are all moments incomplete?

Thank goodness at the time I saw Abe I had supportive supervisors. I was afraid that I was doing something destructive, not at all confident of participating in a creative happening. Often you cannot tell—is this destructive or going to turn out well? Is this something you wait for in hope of a reversal? Even if there is an inkling of birth in progress, what kind of baby would be born? A therapy monster? Therapy is filled with doubt. What happened was a revelation for me as well as Abe. Therapy as revelation, slow hard work that, paradoxically, takes one somewhere one did not know existed, not in a lived way, not for oneself.

Little by little, working with people like Abe, I learned how a melding of faith and catastrophe hold personality together, a double link, mixed ingredients of experience. We like to think therapy shifts the balance, provides new windows, further possibilities of experiencing. As we go through this process and keep going through it, we are not entirely different, yet not entirely the same.

Sometimes when I see what individuals go through, I think of war. In Judaism, there is emphasis on peace in the family. I suspect, in part, because peace is so fragile and elusive. War is something that goes on in and between individuals, families and groups, between and within nations. Aside from practical considerations of power and status, war may also dramatise a basic experience of the human condition. When the background support a baby needs falls apart, the baby falls apart, perhaps experiencing psychic death, strangulated states, various kinds of deformation. Some of this is mended, some one naturally goes through as a sequence, and some becomes part of a pattern of chronic mishap.

War, I fear, attempts to dramatise the damage and death a baby undergoes as part of background failure and loss, mangled, pulverised states that border on loss of life. To put it in a rather extreme but real way, how many people who look put together and well come in for help with horror and hell in the background of their beings? Such states may be mimicked by war in external reality, partly dramatising inner devastation lost to view. A sense of wholeness repeatedly, incessantly, blown up.

Of course, circles of trauma go both ways. From one point of view, what we call peace and war are parts of natural processes. Both visions are ancient, nature as war between elements and balance between interacting tendencies. I do not mean what I am saying as reductionist. Many factors commingle in any situation, including multiple viewpoints. I am merely asking that a particular possibility not be left out: wounds in infancy writ large in war, perhaps so the former can be seen, tasted, undergone. If only dramas of wounded faith in infancy and childhood could form a basis for reflective experience rather than work their ways out in violence, group or individual, a gravitational pull towards the avatar of war. So much goes on in wordless, nameless, thoughtless "subawareness", with profound effects, better and worse.

More recently (2011, Chapter Six), I wrote about phases of recovery of a man with multiple psychotic breaks and hospitalisations. After twelve years of therapy, he was hospital and medication free. Here is another instance of self repeatedly "falling apart" and semiregrouping. After our beginning sessions he took to just sitting in the park or by the river. Nature, just nature. Have any of you had this experience—the importance of being with nature in a peaceful way as part of recovery? Little by little people came into the picture. A sense of "I am" expanding, including nature and now people within its circumference of possibility, first as a waiter and gradually a lover, and, as time went on, creative life unfolded. I felt, too, a kind of unfolding and deepening of body experience, a kind of psyche–body sense, responsive to what touched him in significant ways, a kind of perceptual sensitivity and responsiveness, so that he and his insides grew together: a kind of mutual validation of different levels of experience. Therapy supported meaningful moments of experience that gradually grew.

Question 1:   I wanted to ask about the part in your book where you speak about the miracle of the perforation of the psyche, of the contraction and intensity of experience leading to the perforations. My experience has been that intensity plays a real role in shifts, but my sense is that simply being as present as you can with whatever it is you are experiencing is where shift comes from, simply because we are so absent most of the time that when we actually start to pay attention to our experience we start to recognise that change is what there is, that change is what happens. It's not like suddenly something shifts, it's that suddenly we recognise shift is all that is happening. So I guess my question is: Yes, intensity feels really important for the revolution that you're talking about in Job, but my sense is really what you're talking about is paying attention, paying sharp attention.

Response 1:   Well, we're wonders of plasticity, so there are endless ways to talk about these things and your way is certainly a beautiful way to do that. Whether change is *all* that happens I don't know. I think there is no one thing that happens at any time. So many things are happening all the time and there are so many ways of describing any portion of those things. I have had experiences of all sorts in therapy. I have seen change happen when I wasn't paying attention, as though my paying attention burdened someone and change came when no one was looking. My attention, at best, is intermittent or fluctuating. Maybe fluctuations can be useful in modelling that you can be who you are in lots of different ways and you don't have to be glued or unglued. But I love your description of a process that you have experienced and that is very real.

Question 2:   Well, now I feel blank, but now, first I want to thank you for the joy and illumination of mystery and I also want to offer you two symbols for your *unitydistinction* without a hyphen. There are really two very useful symbols. One is the yin–yang symbol where one is held by the other and one kind of shapes into the other but boundaries are kept. And the other is the Star of David because of the tension of the upwardly rising triangle and the downwardly descending triangle creating something in between ascent and descent that is constant. So I think it's a perfect symbol.

Response 2:   Those are both lovely. One of the most beautiful pictures I have seen of yin–yang is in Rudolf Arnheim's book, *Visual Thinking* (1969). I also thought of Winnicott and Milner's overlapping circles. They portray the mother and the infant as overlapping circles with an area of union and an area of distinction.

Question 3:   At the end of the chapter, you talk about wounded togetherness, and I was hoping that you'd have time to address that.

Response 3:   Wounded togetherness—you have both extremes don't you? You have someone who cannot get out of his bed or leave his apartment and someone who cannot stay alone, you have both ends of the spectrum. Almost as if the two belong together. One imagines devastation organised in different ways and you would have to learn more from the person. André Green (1975) talks about a double anxiety, abandonment–intrusion anxiety, that might be working in different ways in both instances. Is abandonment–intrusion anxiety a single anxiety, a double anxiety, an anxiety that oscillates, dissociates, fuses, splits? In some people it is organised rather rigidly, in others it is chameleon-like. There is also the possibility that at some point they are indistinguishable. Or a kind of undifferentiated catastrophic dread that includes both. Why it might take the form of being people-phobic and/or aloneness-phobic is open for research and thought. It is not without reason that Freud spent a good deal of time thinking about what makes for one kind of symptom expression rather than another and what makes for fixity and diffusion.

Green spoke of four ways of handling abandonment–intrusion anxiety. One is splitting. Klein (1945; Eigen, 1996, 2007) pointed out that splitting can proliferate and, if it proliferates enough, feeling diffuses to such an extent that you lose feeling. One keeps splitting anxiety in order to diminish pain, until feeling is lost through diffusion, thinning out. An agonising conflict here might be to feel or not to feel. In such a case, depending on how much feeling is lost, having a nightmare may be a good thing, portending return of anxiety. Anxiety breaking through the splitting process. Anxiety breaking through attempts to kill it off, a capacity to diminish anxiety gone to extreme. In such an instance, it is possible that breakthrough of anxiety signals the return of affect. A return of the unendurable. Therapy tries to work with what cannot be worked with a bit at a time, gradually building more affect tolerance, tolerance for growth of experience.

The second defence is what Green calls somatic exclusion. One handles the double anxiety by somatisation, for example, hosts of body manifestations are possible, including illness. Exclusion means excluding psyche, substituting soma. In certain ways, psyche and soma are capable of reversible relations, either substituted for the other. We think of psyche–soma as one, or aspects of a complex field or fields, with variable relationships between parts of fields possible. Intolerance of what we mean by psyche can put too much pressure on the body. The body is forced to work overtime to compensate for psychic failure or incapacity.

A third mode of responding to abandonment–intrusion anxiety is by acting out, externalising it. To sum up, you have acting in, acting out, splitting, and the fourth is the most devastating of all, a severely schizoid defence Green calls *decathexis*.

In psychosis, Freud writes of withdrawal of libido from object to the ego, resulting in ego inflation, megalomania. One protects oneself from the object by hyper-inflating the ego, emphasising narcissism, grandiosity. Green goes further, emphasising loss of feeling for self as well as reality. Decathexis, withdrawal of libido or energy or interest, is not only from the object, but from the subject as well. It is not just that the reality of the other is lost. The reality of the self is lost. This coheres with the emphasis by Winnicott on depersonalisation as well as derealisation. It is not simply the world that is unreal, I am unreal. Loss of self-feeling. My "I" does not feel its own realness. This might sound like a moment on the path to enlightenment and certainly is an experience that has been expressed by many since antiquity. But here it is awful, forcing the person away from meaningful participation in his or her own life. A radical withdrawal from life itself.

For one who has to be alone, there could be fear of losing any remnant of self that is left by exposing oneself to external cruelty. As Sartres said, in such a moment, others are hell. At the same time, a person who cannot be alone might be using the other as a defence against the anxiety of disappearing. In this case, one needs aloneness not to disappear; in another, one needs people in order not to disappear. For one, being with people increases anxiety, for the other, being with people reduces anxiety. Decathexis swings both ways. Sometimes the object is more real, sometimes less real. Sometimes the self is more real, sometimes less real. Look for how one is protecting the self from a more complete decathexis. If you decathect everything, nothing is left, not a creative, positive, pulsating nothing, but a ghastly nothing. Why be alive? Perhaps some people continue being alive in that state because they cathect the decathexis. The decathexis becomes an identity feeling.

Question 4:   In the case of Abe, where everyone was cheering him when he was happy and down when he was down, it makes me think of Saint John of the Cross saying that the blessing is hidden in the affliction and the affliction is hidden in the blessing. He says that when we feel blessed we feel it is going to last forever and when we feel down we feel that it is going to last forever. I think that it is very difficult to get out of this feeling, I am familiar with feeling when things go well—oh, it will last; then when things don't go well—oh, it will last too. You talk about silence and waiting, but how to feel both at the same time, not to know—but how to *feel* it is the question.

Response 4:   As you hint, it is easier to think it than to feel it. Let me reverie. It is a terrific dilemma. Of course, we are all in it. Rumi says something similar to what Saint John says: the cure for the pain is in the pain.

I spoke earlier of transcendent vision, something of an even keel while an emotional storm is going on. A transcendent attitude that takes in the full curve of a situation (at least a little better than other-wise) and makes some room for dual states and their progressions. One moment ah, good, one moment uhhh, terrible. You might get to see/feel that the two states go together, perhaps even belong together. States oscillate and are mixed. It won't come as such a surprise when good turns to bad or bad to good, although surprise and shock might be part of the experience. You might think such an attitude is too intel-lectualised, and that can be the case. But it can strike deep, connecting one to a sense of reality deeper than the immediate conflict.

For example, the *Tanya* (Zalman, 1797) asks, what about a Chassid who does not have a burning affect, does not have a fervour for God, but loves God? Loves God, but does not have the fire in his gut. Rabbi Schneur Zalman makes room for this type. One can reach God in a more mentalised way, perhaps something like Spinoza's *amor dei*. A more intellectual level of God or vision of God or sense of God. There is room for many ways to God. Not everyone has heat, not everyone has to burn. Thinking can be good enough to keep on a faith track, a mitzvah track.

Is good enough good enough? Put the two types together, the cool and the hot. Suppose they are in one person and the person has to learn to make room for such changes or variations in his souls. Such a person might be in conflict with himself, too hot, too cold. What kind of a person am I? Suppose these states are divided up between different people. There can be antagonism, depreciation, misunderstanding between warmer and cooler souls. How does one grow to make room for various souls and temperaments in others and oneself? Too often, souls fight rather than co-operate (for an intense meditation on Dostoevsky's two souls, see Berdyaev, 1958).

Chassidus–Kabbalah teaches there are five souls. There are probably more, but today we will emphasise three. They correspond with different capacities and tendencies and suggest that we live with mixed natures. Learning to use the array of tendencies that inhabit us is no small task. What a difference it makes whether souls are at war or peace within and between themselves.

Nefesh is the vital soul on the plane of Malchut, the tenth *Sephira*, the earthly plane, action, everyday life (Eigen, 2012a; Figure 1, p. 3). *Ruach*, breath, spirit, is an emotional soul. It spans *Sephirot* 4–9, *Chesed* (mercy), *Gevurah* (judgement, strength, severity), *Tiferet* (beauty), *Netzach* (perseverance), *Hod* (flexibility), *Yesod* (foundation, sexuality). There are other ways to break this down, other dimensions one can emphasise. You can divide these six *sephirot* into lower and higher emotions, so to speak. The lower triangle *netzach–hod–yesod* and the higher triangle *chesed–gevurah–tiferet* have broad correspondences to *chakras*: sacral, solar plexus, heart. There are inexhaustible intricacies, some of which perhaps we can take up another time.

Neshama is a still higher soul comprising intellectual–intuitive functions. It involves the triangle *Keter* (will, grace, faith, humility), *Chochma* (wisdom), *Binah* (understanding), *Sephirot* 1-3. It can also be made up of a lower triangle: *Chochma* (wisdom), *Binah* (understanding), *Daat* (knowledge, a hidden dimension, which is uncounted in the usual ten *sephirot*).

The ten *sephirot* are called the Tree of Life. In practical terms, it is modelled on the human body, or an idealised body: head–neck (intellect–intuition), arms–chest–abdomen–genitals–hips–legs (emotion–sensation), feet (action). It links with ancient models. For example, Aristotle's souls, from lower vegetative (nutritive), animal (sensitive), through higher rational intellectual. Plato has similar divisions. And there are resonances in Buddhist and Hindu texts. In more recent times, you can see parallels in Jung's four functions (intuition, intellect, feeling, sensation) or Husserl's empirical, psychological and transcendental egos, or Kierkegaard's man of action, aesthetics, ethics, spirit (religion). In practice, the relations between the *sephirot* are fluid, each *sephira* containing all the others. Each soul containing all others.

There is so much more to say. Here, I at least want to mention two still higher souls. *Chaya* is above the *sephirot*. There are infinite supernal realms or dimensions beyond the *sephirot* in all "directions". *Chaya* is a life source above. In Kabbalah, life comes from above. The Tree of Life has roots in Godly Infinity. A link between *Chaya* and *Keter* is part of infinite intimate fluidity.

Still "higher" is *Yechida*, which unites our essence with God's essence. If you think of the *Sephirot*, the Tree of Life, you have to think of it against an Infinite Background which permeates and sustains it. The *sephirot* are depicted as divine functions, modes of distillations for godly energies, which is a kind of archetypal background for our use of these capacities on our earthly plane. We are free to explore the earth in all its glories, intricacies, difficulties, horrors, possibilities, at the same time at any moment, in *all* moments, exercise of our capacities and gifts and being are parts of divine presence. That contact, that intimacy–distance, can be explored with our capacities as well. Another kind of logic is at work here. All dimensions are inside and outside each other.

The basic form of these models involves verticality, above–below, higher–lower, probably related to the upright posture. Think of all the meanings upright has, related to right, righteousness, righting oneself when off balance, others you can come up with—all with implications for a higher–lower binary or continuum which informs thinking. In yoga, the spine's uprightness is a vertical vehicle for energy flows and blocks and emphasis is placed on lower and higher functions in society, interpersonally and individually.

A vertical model has strengths and limitations. To try to squeeze all of our feeling–sensation life into a vertical model does not make sense. In experience, feeling can be more like spreads, whirls, jumbles, intertwining, permeating, squishy, wriggly stuff. I have heard it said that there are no straight lines in nature. It appears that uprightness exerts some pressure towards straight-line thinking. Proprioception, synaesthesia, kinaesthesia, spreads and swirls of sensations evade a more upright stereotype as the only model. In–out (e.g., respiration, digestion, sexual intercourse) can have important links with verticality, but the latter does not exhaust the former. Similarly, feeling spreads of meaning, being permeable to meaning flows, elusive intimations—modern painting and music come close to expressing wiggles, curves, interpenetration–exclusion, fusions of forms and hints of forms in rippling, suggestive, hard to pin down ways.

In Kabbalah, the higher you get, the closer to God you are. *Yechida* is the closest of all. Even in heaven, there are some souls closer to God than others. Even among the saints, there is a closeness–distance continuum, although here we are speaking of grades of closeness. But, as Rabbi Nachman testifies, to a *tzadik*, even a little distance from God can be agonising, so much is the closest closeness desired (Eigen, 2012a, Chapter Two).

The descending order of *sephirot* belong to different worlds as well as souls. Loosely speaking, *Keter* (crown) straddles higher supernal realities as it acts as a funnel for the nine *sephirot* under it. This higher reality, closer to the divinity of divinity, is called emanation, minimum separation from the Source. In an informal sense, all the *sephirot* are Godly emanations, but they are divided along a closeness–distance spectrum. *Keter* is part of the world of emanation, and *Chaya* a higher life-soul. The second realm involves the "head" *sephirot*, *Chochma* and *Binah* (and the hidden *Daat*), world of creation and the *neshama* soul. The third realm involves the middle group, the emotive *sephirot*, world of formation and the *ruach* soul. The fourth realm involves *Malchut*, the last *sephira*, world of action and the *nefesh* soul.

If all these functions, worlds, souls are parts of Divinity, it appears that Divinity can have a closer and more distant relation to itself. There can be infinite dimensions of divinity, the divine of the divine. Yet, we also say God is One. We are at a partial loss. We wade into mystery at the edge of mystery. We understand we are speaking of ourselves, our cognitive, emotional, and instinctual capacities. Our picture of God as a projection of our makeup. And yet we cannot rest with that. A projection, yet . . . Kabbalah itself goes beyond itself and, as most mystics do, recognises a domain of unknowing and intimacy closer to ourselves than we are, through which there seems no end to Unknown Intimacy.

The idea of near–far is part of Asian as well as Western thinking. I once heard D. T. Suzuki give a talk about seven heavens in Buddhism.

Seven heavens is a familiar theme. In a less formal way, Dante gives expression to something like this in *Paradiso*. Beatrice moves from one heaven to another. The more she enters divine reality, the more divine reality there is, unfolding wave after heavenly wave.

At a certain level of experience, East and West have their versions of a merit system. If you accumulate more merits, you add to your chance of a better outcome. Perhaps the outcome is a higher level of life, with all its challenges, or a higher place in heaven. In the latter case, good and evil is rewarded by nearness–distance from God. One can imagine that the same person can be at once near to and far from God as a function of good and bad elements. In that regard, the World to Come can vary from moment to moment. The World to Come as the next moment—or now.

Every system has many resources. Each may include a merit system but also have ways of going beyond it, terms like Nirvana or Grace. We are more or other than the sum of our merits and faults. In Kabbalah, in *yechida*, the soul point in contact with God is pure. To taste that soul, that point of contact, is its own reward, ineffable bliss beyond good and evil.

Kabbalah also teaches that the lowest level, *Malchut, nefesh*, action, is also the most important in its way. It is the world of our everyday experience where struggle, learning or failure to learn, and soul dramas go on. The logic that the good are closer to God now and in heaven has a domain of reversibility. There is a domain in which God is less worried about the good than the bad. If you are near to God now, you will be near to God in the World to Come. But what we really need is the reverse. What of those who are far—how can they come close? God wants the bad to come close, to find a way. A repentant sinner may be closer to God than one with a better nature to start with. There are many ways to sin and there is such a thing as sinning bringing one closer to God. One may feel God all the closer, the further from God one is. Some of the most moving passages in the Bible involve the soul becoming white as snow where it once seemed unredeemable. How can the soul within be pure when one is so corrupt? Is one both? Are there shifts back and forth, simultaneity of worlds?

When I was studying with two old men in Crown Heights, Brooklyn, many years ago, they told me Hell is not what you think it is. It is like going to the cleaners. The soul gets cleaned up so it can go to heaven.

An ideal vision is that there will be no evil or death. No evil or death. The fact of evil and death should make us more loving with each other and ourselves. Too often it spurs competitiveness, hierarchical thinking. Even in Buddhism competing schools and teachers have led to violence. Who is more enlightened than whom? Whose path is truer? Even the Way becomes persecutory, a pecking order of superior and inferior.

Does quality and degree of enlightenment or closeness–farness from God vary? Suppose I feel my portion is enough. One day my cup runneth over. Another moment it is half empty or nearly empty, or, if possible, entirely empty. Today it is filled only a tiny bit—I can hardly feel it. Sometimes I cannot feel it at all. Yet, I can feel in any of these states that my portion is enough. Do I have to wait until destruction and death vanish or are vanquished to be truly happy? I suspect with the kinds of minds we have, even that would not be enough. Perhaps we harbour a heroic element that cannot rest until all this destruction and horror is undone. Then we will get down to business.

It is a challenge of *Malchut* to reach this state in the midst of destruction and horror. To do the work here and now. To be truly free here and now. What is freedom but a Moment of Grace? The freedom of Faith, the intimacy of Faith. A sure way to shut this possibility down is to insist on hierarchical, persecutory merit—who is better, what is better. The good go to heaven, the bad to hell, reward and punishment. Nothing shuts down Grace like righteousness. On the other side of the spectrum, in an extreme moment, in the depths of my unredeemable state, totally without hope or possibility, closeness to divinity arises, closeness beyond belief. Contact in the depths of hopeless longing. Such moments make me wonder if God isn't always equally close to everyone.

The *sephirot*, the five souls and four worlds encompass so many human capacities, work together so many ways. They can be co-nourishing, dissociated, blocked, antagonistic, work against each other and themselves, or open worlds of possibility, worlds of living. And we can go beyond them, through them, touch a sense no description of capacity comes close to encompassing. We can go past capacities that constitute us and capacities yet to be born, and in some way we cannot identify, taste the Unborn, Allborn, Everborn. As it says of God in the prayers, "There is none else". And yet, this *None Else* gives us all there is. Heavens of taste.

I suppose I am speaking of a moment without limitations, or a moment in which limits do not matter or do not get in the way of something else one might be tempted to call unlimited. Perhaps it is closer to it to say that another domain opens up in which something else happens, something for which we lack adequate descriptive tools. Bion (1994b; Eigen, 2012a) repeatedly tells us that what is intimated cannot be described in articulate speech, that none of the formulations of religion are up to describing what they are trying to call attention to.

Still, coming down to earth, I would like to call attention to a sensation in the background of our beings. We have a background body sensation that goes all through our bodies, all through us, if it is unblocked even a little. It is a wonderful feeling. A background feeling sensation all through us or, rather, more densely focused in some places than others. Sometimes it can be a God-sensation, sometimes not. It is mute, just is. Moments of being quietly happy. Can one break it down through analysis?

One can analyse almost anything. When one analyzes something, one finds multiple possibilities. The more one looks, the more is there. For example, in psychosis, someone may hear God saying, "You can only go to Heaven if you kill your friend" or whoever or whatever is named, perhaps children in a school or a man in the subway or someone in one's own home. The voice can tell one to randomly kill whoever appears in one's field of view or someone in one's life. The voice can set it up so that the person fears that if he does not follow it, he will go to hell forever. He will feel he lacks courage to follow the voice wherever it leads. He will fail God and himself, even if the voice commands him to jump in front of a train.

In therapy we look closer. Who is speaking? Is this God? The devil? In *The Psychotic Core* (1986), I write of a moment in which I tell someone, "You have God and the devil mixed up." This is not an idea that would normally occur to someone in this hapless circumstance, but it often happens, I suspect, that God and the devil are mixed up in our minds. Soon after I said this, the person began seeing devils. Some people looked more like devils than others. He was frightened to see devils nearly everywhere. He was caught between the devils he saw and God's voice that he heard inside. A terrible conflict, but it threw some doubt on God's commands.

A next step in therapy was encouraging him to stare at the devils and say what he saw. Just keep staring. There are spiritual exercises where you stare into space or at your face in a mirror in the darkness with a candle burning. Just keep staring and say what you see, only in this case it was staring at devils. What do you see? The more you look the more you start to see.

After repeated efforts over weeks, the man said, "I see my father, my father in his angry mode. I see my father raging at me. My father looks like a devil. The devil looks like my father." It is not that he stops seeing devils, but now in the devil he also sees an image of his father. A little like multiple colours and quivers of the light of a flame. If you look closely, different forms appear but the flame is still a flame. After more time, this man began to see himself in the devils as well. "I see my own mutilated ego. A strangulated, mutilated I—my face, an image of my face that looks like a devil. My own I, my own face is the devil."

An important component of his emergent experience was a sense that somewhere his body did not want to die. Something in him did not want to kill others or himself. He was afraid to die, to kill. He recoiled from killing life. These fears and sensations were put aside as being cowardly. They would keep him from following the commands of the voice. Yet, as time went on, we began to see his body fears and inklings as another reality that had a right to have a say, and this reality was pro-life. This reality wanted to live and foster life.

So, we can deconstruct the devil over time and see components that make up this particular devil. There are countless devils, endless demons, but each looks a little different and has a different story, a different history to tell. I learnt about this in the Frick Museum in New York City many years ago. At an exhibit I saw a particular painting of a devil and when I saw this devil, I said—that's my devil, that's it, that's "me". An immediate sense of recognition. I learnt a lot about this devil over the years. So, when I saw my patient, I was curious. "What does your devil look like? Tell me all you can about what you see?" With coaxing and encouraging support, the thing that seemed so fixed and immutable began to have a process, a process made up of many processes. Something steadfast, but also something shifting and changing.

Question 5:   There's a Tibetan practice called *Chud*, which means to cut, and *Chud* practitioners will go into the graveyards and they feed the ghosts, and there is a contemporary—actually she's one of my teachers, Lama Tsultrim Allione—who has taken this practice and translated it for Westerners. Her book is called *Feeding Your Demons* and what she teaches is a five-part practice in which I survey my body and look at what's eating at me. For example, right now I'm a little hungry, I have a stomach-ache, so, rather than push it away, I feed it, I go into that entity. I give it a colour and a shape and I ask it three questions: What do you want? What do you need? And how will you feel when you get it? And then I answer as that demon. Rather than trying to exorcise or eradicate, I feed that which is clamouring to be seen.

Response 5:   Thank you. You bring out the importance of getting to know and feed our hungry demons. At the moment what comes to mind is Rabbi Nachman when he would travel (Eigen, 2012a, Chapter Two). One of the stops he always made was at local cemeteries. He would see hungry souls between life and death, or in various death processes, or processes of being stuck after death. He would spend a good deal of time praying for the souls he saw. It is not exactly feeding them but it is close.

Before time is up, I would like to mention three dimensions of life, which roughly correspond to different souls or soul regions. The first is *just plain me*. Just plain us. I remember a beer commercial I saw years ago. A man is sitting at a bar, everyone talking, having a good time. The bartender asks him what kind of beer he wants. All of a sudden the man is hurled out of the bar into space. He is gone, gone, very gone . . . and suddenly the scene snaps back into place and he is back on planet Earth, in the bar, a look of secret relief. Those who know what it is like to hurtle far beyond your ordinary self to unknown spaces, then come back, will recognise the look of relief— I'm back, just plain me. Finally, the man orders his beer, Bud Light, and the bar scene comes back to life. So much happened in just a micro-moment, hurtling through other worlds. What a relief to be back.

I personally would not want to get away from just plain us too quickly. I really like just plain us light, just breathing, hanging out, looking at faces, walking down the street, doing nothing. Perhaps we could locate "just plain us" in aspects of Malchut and the *nefesh* soul, although such correspondence is very loose.

Then there is a second realm that I call the sacrificial, penitential realm. A realm of constant struggle with my faults, flaws, evils, sins—

struggle with ways I hurt people, my patients, my wife, my children, myself—constant struggle with what is wrong with me. I might locate constant struggle in aspects of the middle *sephirot*, the *ruach* soul.

We tend to under-or-overdo the need to struggle with ourselves. At one point, people called it struggling with sin. Freud took away sin and gave us psychopathology, struggling with madness or neurosis or other psychic constellations. Now there are movements that want to depathologise the psyche, perhaps mute the need to struggle with destructive tendencies. We can attempt to depathologise destruction but, sooner or later, the human race will have to struggle with its destructive tendencies. There are individuals who have tried to do this and are trying now, attempting to learn how to work with tendencies that constitute us. You cannot wish destructive tendencies away, they have to be wrestled with, and we often are not up to the job. We are plagued not only with destruction aimed at others but ways we wound ourselves. There are ancient Greek sculptures where struggle is not represented—all seems in balance, harmony, beautiful. But there are other statues in which struggle is represented, enormous effort pitted against great odds, for example, a giant serpent. In struggle with the gods and Fate one senses, too, struggle with oneself. What is wrong with me? My evil, self-defeating nature?

A third state I would like to emphasise I am calling a Grace dimension. When Saint Paul says he is in a state of grace, he says he does not know where he is or what he is, whether he has a body, or even mind in a usual sense. He is transported beyond usual faculties, peace that passeth understanding. In such a moment you don't ask questions about the nature of existence. You reach a place beyond questions and habitual maps. You are in a wonderful state of grace. A moment beyond or outside of dualities. Of this "place" or moment (one of the Hebrew names for God is *Hamakom*—the Place), Saint Augustine says, "Love and do what you will". One could link this state with the higher *sephirot* and the *neshama* soul, or beyond the *sephirot*, the *chaya* and yechida souls, the last soul essence linked with Godly essence.

Just plain me; penitential struggle; grace. Three phases, dimensions, successive or simultaneous, three moments or tendencies operative in a variety of ways at any time. Religion often divides these soul moments up into realms such as heaven, purgatory, and—not hell, as just plain me is the earth self, middle earth. Upper, middle, lower.

There are many "contradictions" in religions and individuals, wherever one finds oneself. For example, one of Rabbi Nachman's obsessions was that he should not get pleasure from sex (Eigen, 2012a, Chapter Two). Getting pleasure from sex would put him on a lower plane. On the other hand, pleasure from sex is part of the *mitzvah*. But if you want to be holier still and get a closer room to God in the World to Come (or, simply, be closer to God), you do a *mitzvah* for its own sake, not for pleasure. We get into conundrums here, since pleasure can be an intrinsic part of a *mitzvah*, pleasure in performing a *mitzvah*. For someone like Nachman, being even a tiny bit away from God is terribly painful. In his mind, you are closer to God when you do a *mitzvah* for its own sake. The experience of intense erotic pleasure bringing you closer to God seems another world.

There are similar ideas in parts of Buddhism. So many *sutras* are like Platonic dialogues in their own way—formalised, sometimes fabulous and idealised. We probably do not know what Buddha said and can, at best, only make guesses. One story seems to show fallibility of judgement, even Buddha's. Buddha spent a lot of time in the community but liked to meditate alone in forests. In the Middle East, deserts. In Asia, mountains and forests. Teaching was important. Aloneness was important. In one de-idealising story, Buddha goes off to a solitary retreat and instructs his disciples to make a corpse the focus of their attention while he is gone. When he came back, there were many fewer disciples. Some killed themselves, some left. They could not take watching a putrid corpse and bear repulsion at the decay process. Some practitioners handled it. They opened to death and death opened them (Blomfield, 2011).

This reminds me a little of the Rabbi Akiva story about going into the garden. Four men go into the garden (Kabbalah, Eden, aspects of the soul). One kills himself, one goes mad, one becomes a heretic, and Rabbi Akiva comes out glowing. The Buddha story shows Buddha's judgement is not infallible. He lost men, strengthened others. The Akiva story touches the issue of varying capacity to tolerate mystical experience. What are we ready for? What can we handle?

In the story of Buddha and the corpse, Buddha did not comment on the men who were lost but kept on with the disciples that remained. This story reminds me of Freud telling Jung, when a disciple killed himself, we lose a lot of good men. But the movement did not hesitate.

Here is another seemingly similar instance. A disciple who was absent for a while explained he slept with his wife to impregnate her, so that he could leave progeny. Buddha reportedly told him, "Better to have put your penis in the burning embers, or in the mouth of a cobra, than in a vagina" (Blomfield, 2011, p. 198). Rather dramatic, but with similarity to Nachman's need to tear out erotic pleasure by its roots, pleasure expressive of a lower level on the spiritual ladder.

Let me balance these negatives with a happier story. Buddha goes into a forest to meditate. His disciples try to warn him that a killer/thief inhabits the forest. Buddha, wanting contact with the depths, enters the forest more deeply. Sure enough, the robber-murderer walks after him. Buddha goes deeper, further, keeping the same pace, yet the man must run to try to keep up with him. The man runs and runs but cannot seem to get to him. Finally, Buddha stops and faces him. He tells the man, "The reason you can't reach me is you are running too fast and I'm much slower than you." The man immediately becomes Buddha's disciple and stops being a thief and murderer (Blomfield, 2011, p. 246).

In the Nachman/Buddha sexual stories, we seem to be approaching a penitential struggle dimension. The moment the thief recognises his deeper nature is akin to a moment of grace. I would say, too, there are pleasure moments of many kinds that open a gate of Grace.

*   *   *

I'd like to comment briefly on the distinction–union structure which runs through our dualities. Dualities are connected in their distinctness and distinct in their connectedness. Often we say of extremes or opposites, "They are two sides of a coin." A student of mine for many years was fond of saying, "Extremes meet."

We have difficulty making room for coexisting states, many-sided simultaneities. Binaries are in varied relationships with each other. They can be experienced as oscillating, antagonistic, reversible, symbiotic, co-nourishing, fused, parallel, indistinguishable. They can organise into more or less enduring patterns of relationships. In the Schreber case, Freud (1911c) wrote about reversible relationships between love and hate, one signifying the other, substituting for the other, defending against the other. He also wrote about reversible pronouns. I can be you, you me in the symmetrical mode of being. The idea of feeding the demon—we can feed each other's demons or our

own. Through work and vision we can enter co-nourishing relationships with what seems to be destroying us. Needless to say, it does
not always work so well. Too often, we are co-destructive rather than
co-nourishing. But perhaps we can find better mixtures and tip the
balance. Sometimes the outcome hinges on a mixture of creative
feeling and *kavanna*, devotion, sincerity, faith. A faith that can wait,
a hope that the faith side, the co-nourishing side will eventually
outweigh co-destructiveness. States fuse and dissociate, split and
meld. We work with so many so-called dualities: mind–body,
spirit–matter, love–hate—all interconnected with each other, bobbing
up in different places in a common sea.

Sometimes we feel more here than others, sometimes all here.
Sometimes we feel we are at the place we have to be now and sometimes feel we will never get there. We might feel we are always fail-
ing to come into being and at other times feel we are there, as fully as
possible. Recently, I watched part of the film, *The Titanic*, the earlier,
not the later one. At the end, you see people dying all kinds of deaths,
no one way to die, no one way to realise this is it. All kinds of ways
to defend or transcend or something more elusive. I was especially
touched by the band playing as the ship went down. A moment of the
big tree, the Faith tree. What do you play as the ship goes down?
William Blake's wife described the way he sang joyously as he died.
Steve Jobs is reported to have said, "Wow . . . Wow" as he was dying.

A few days after I saw *The Titanic*, I saw part of *One Flew Over the
Cuckoo's Nest*. There is so much to say about it. Right now I am thinking about Billy, whose mother was a friend of Big Nurse, Nurse
Ratched. Billy was under Nurse Ratched's care. The character played
by Jack Nicholson, sort of a psychopath, in this context a vital life
figure, landed in the hospital and tried to liven things up. He brought
in prostitutes and Billy lost his virginity, deliriously happy. He had
chronically stuttered and after this night stopped stuttering.

When Big Nurse found out, she shamed him, saying something
like, "How could you do this? What am I going to tell your mother?"
She was unyielding. You saw his spirit dropping, dropping, dropping, until he couldn't speak any more. Then he killed himself. And
soon the life figure played by Jack Nicholson was made lifeless by
brain damaging electric shock.

In one or another way, this drama goes on all the time. The
band playing as the ship goes down. Loss or destruction of faith after

something good happens and the reverse. I was redeemed but now am lost. I was lost but now am redeemed. Such states could be tied to the rise and fall of the feeling of aliveness. Now I feel more alive, now less, now I enter variable realms of deadness and so many shifting mixtures. We sometimes express this by saying the spirit lives, the spirit dies, and all the gradations and revelations of aliveness-deadness (Eigen, 1996).

Religions often express this drama in their imagery and narratives, dramas of shifting aliveness and its forms. Now I am dead. Now I live. Jonah has much in common with Jesus. Three days in the great fish's belly, then out into life, paralleled by Jesus in the tomb three days followed by resurrection. Kabbalah says that Jonah died in the big fish, a transitional moment. Remember, he was at sea in a storm, hiding at the bottom of the ship, his spirit already dead or dying, evading its calling. "I don't want to be a prophet. I don't want to have a baby. I don't want to risk all I am." Prophecy is terrible. You might say, a penitential struggle is at work between the prophet and common sense, between a higher calling and the everyday self.

Perhaps an acme of a penitential moment is when Jonah says, "Throw me into the sea. I am the problem." Yes—we are the problem. How do we rise to the challenge of our own natures? Jonah died and came back to life. He passed through an emotional storm of revelation. His nature throughout the story, like all Biblical characters, was mixed. His "redemption" was not perfect. He was still a flawed creature with much work ahead. But he passed through a death and met his task, to the extent he could, and saved a city by his appearance and words.

We can view the whole story as a drama within one personality. The city is the city of our own self. We are speaking to ourselves, urging ourselves towards repentance, renewal, change. We are urging ourselves towards a better life. I doubt every bit of us will repent, begin anew, enter a growth process. Some will stay behind, inert, set in ways, cemented by habit and will. Perhaps a few more will shift and join in a fuller movement in the future. Meanwhile, we work with what we have, a little more than before.

If the Grace Jonah experienced was flawed, it was still a taste with significant consequences. Tastes of Grace—what a way to go through life! In Jonah's case and our own, tastes of Grace and bitterness. I would like to speak more about the "saving storm" that could dash us to pieces, dash the bitterness to pieces, the outcome never certain (Eigen, 2005), but I see we are running out of time.

Even a prophet like Jonah is a mixture of yes and no, fear and vision. More broadly, a mixture between the *rasha* (evil one) and *tzadik* (wise one) parts of us. The storm comes, the fish eats us up, we die, we come alive. To be buried and then live. There are stories of someone being dead most of his or her life, then coming alive at the last moment, nearly one's whole life a grave, then a moment of grace. How Jonah must have battled with his inner accuser, with God, the movement of Jonah's being both accusing and propelling, brakes pressed, accelerator on, stuck between towards–away.

Yet, he comes alive, does his job. He lives in light of God's mercy even as a partly failed *tzadik*, the journey a kind of variation of what I call a rhythm of faith. Whatever our level and capacity, we die in spirit, we come back. Theory postulates a complete *tzadik*, one whose victory over the evil inclination is so thorough, the latter is turned to good. But, in reality, we are at best incomplete, mixed, stymied, busy at work with what oppresses us, perhaps in partial despair, partly inspired.

Perhaps a meaning of the saying that a *rasha*, a bad person, can be closer to God than a complete *tzadik* has to do with spending more time in the belly and bowels of the fish, the furnace, before the turn came. More baking time heightens appreciation. I suspect in a lifetime we go through all these states and many more. We go through these realms on a daily basis, moment to moment, month to month, more in the fish, more just plain me, more struggle, more grace.

Our vanishing and coming back, decathexis–cathexis—our nature scares us. Psychotherapy helps us stay with these fluctuations, helps us bear more of the twists and turns of our feelings. Like Jonah, imperfectly. But as part of a path, a direction. How much of ourselves can we tolerate, how much of ourselves can we enjoy, sometimes lightly, and sometimes a depth that brings tears.
(Applause)

Question 6:   I have a question about Abe and the I-centre in his chest. What I like about your presentation is you didn't take the easy way out. You didn't let the fact that we are interactive obscure the importance of the finding of the I, a coming alive of the I in a special way, the I itself, just it, as it is. In this case, a greater I. An I-sense for the moment without versus, not I *vs.* other, just I. A coming alive of a presence in the world naturally finding the language of I. Not an inherently separate I *vs.* enlightened Buddha not-I. You stayed with the I-feeling that emerged—and that really is about listening. Listening to an awareness coming into being much larger than I as little I.

Response 6:   Letting be, sustaining are words that come. Why do religions emphasise hierarchies and binaries, pitting this against that? I suspect one reason has to do with premature closure, incapacity to stay with processes and letting them develop. So many binaries may be premature formulations, closing off as complete, done, what is still in process. Odd to call formations that are thousands of years old premature. It is as if they felt an impact then precociously formulated it into ethical hierarchical systems. I think right now, at this point of history, some of these formulations get in the way. Maybe you can pick and choose what you can and can't use, what speaks to you or how you can reformulate treasured lights so that they facilitate rather than hold you back on your particular journey. Or they might pick and choose you, gravitate towards you, reach you. Old formulations are wonderful to tap into and can lead to realities you might not touch without them. But it is also good to take them with a grain of salt if you find yourself spinning through them into destructive binds. Letting the "original" impact grow rather than close off with decisions made long ago as to what is being structured and how. What is the impact, impacts, or Impact that lead to religious feeling? The vicissitudes of that feeling are still ongoing now and we are called to address it in our way. Millions of hands on millions of elephants, infinite infinities, and a thread runs through them.

Question 7:   In my understanding, mystical experience occurs in the context of a discipline of soul, body, and mind which I feel we neglected a little bit today or in general nowadays. Spontaneous expression of self now seems to take precedence over a less free, more constrained, restrictive discipline and practice of religion that is less individualistic but provides a context for the spiritual to emerge. It's not just if you do *mitzvahs* you're saved and if you don't you're damned. I feel in the experience of every *mitzvah* there's an opportunity for a connection, a chance to get closer to God. Out of the *mitzvahs* a person may do by rote, there is opportunity with the right *kavannah* [devotion, intention] for them to become a vehicle for present spiritual experience. It's not just about the outcomes created for the world to come but the hallowing of the moment that is. Mundane washing of the hands before bread, let us say, presents opportunity to experience closeness to *Hashem* [The Name, the Holy One] that is in and of itself rewarding. Even if you end up going to *Gehenna*, God forbid, or anything else that happens—you have this close moment to *Hashem*.

Response 7:   Well, that provides a good balance. I totally agree that there is inherent meaning in so much traditional practice and that the discipline can be releasing. There is, too, the vision of *mitzvahs* taking one closer to God. I think the matter is very individual. I respect and support its working for you. It has potential not just to purify and lift one to another level, but to be a source of intimacy with the Divine in its own right. It is good that you emphasise intrinsic intimacy that observance mediates, although being orthodox didn't work for me. I have had to find my own way with a kind of spiritual smorgasbord. I'm a patchwork. But I feel resonance with what you are saying and your emphasis on the positive aspect of the *mitzvah* now, the spiritual aspect of religious practice. I reverberate with what you are saying even though we have our differences in practice.

When I was younger, I would often hear it is important not to be eclectic but to go deeply in your particular path. If you were Catholic, be a fuller Catholic. If you were a Jew or Buddhist, be that with all you have. Whatever your practice, there's more than enough for you to develop. They all have endless depths and heights and lots between. Through the hardships of life, I discovered that I'm eclectic. A bad word where I come from. I've had to make the best of it. That doesn't mean that I don't live the just plain, everyday me, and the penitential and grace realms in my own particular style. I work the farm I've been given as I can. There is no one way to touch and be touched by The Great Light.

It is not just in religions that there are premature closures of impact. One of the hardest things in a psychoanalytic seminar is to support students in hearing each other and respecting each other's truths, their different ways of formulating experience. So often one or another feels their way is right or more right than the others. A microcosm of battles of truth in the larger world, which often take one away from grappling with how life feels, how it *can* feel.

But thank you, thank you. I like to encourage each of us to mine the tracks we are on. The paths that open as we live. There are quirks I have developed as I've gone along. For example, if I do a Jewish service, I have given myself permission not to gallop along. If a phrase ambushes me, I might stay with that silently a long time, let it do its work. I remember a service I attended in Jerusalem and another in Tsfat that, compared to most in New York, seemed in slow motion. It was as if words vanished or became doors and all that was left was *kavanna*. At other times, a word might light me up or have profound meaning that grows over time. You never know what will bring you where, what will undo and redo you, at least in part. For me, the tradition (there are many variants) is a vital resource, but I do not buy the whole package. I guess what I am saying is I support you in your way and myself in mine.

Mitzvahs can be a pipeline to God. For others an obstruction. For the same person, they can function as amazing resources and psychospiritual strangulation. I am thinking of a patient whose father became orthodox in her later childhood with near fanatic zeal. So much of life had to do with what was and wasn't allowed. She gained a lot from religious feeling and rituals, yet became more and more tormented. As she grew into young womanhood, the torment began to spiral. In one instance, a conflict arose between whether or not to go to a dear friend's wedding. The wedding was going to be in a Reformed temple, which was forbidden. Her father told her not to go. It was a painful situation that grew worse. There are treasures and undo constrictions in every belief system. She decided not to go to her friend's wedding and felt horrible about that. But had she gone, she'd probably have felt horrible about that, too. Such conflicts are written large in cases of psychosis, where the tension between good and bad spirals out of all proportion. Nothing like psychosis happened with my patient, but the situation left a bad taste in her being. I would like to think that with the work we did over time, she might feel a little freer now in such a situation. She has made many modifications in the practice of her faith that enabled her to grow as a person and in spirit.

Question 8:   I want to ask you more about your devil. You said that Bion's Faith in O might be akin to faith in various religions. I'm curious about those who do believe in a devil as an oppositional force as opposed to an openness. I'm curious in a psychoanalytic therapeutic session do you see times when opposition, as opposed to openness, is appropriate?

Response 8:   Ah, the psychoanalyst as devil. Opposition is how the psyche, the I, is partly structured. The psyche is oppositional to a certain extent. Distinction–union can have opposing and union aspects, with need to evolve both. William Blake has some of the best expressions of the devil as a creative force in a book called *The Marriage of Heaven and Hell*. He wrote of the devil as a source of energy and energy as eternal delight. In this case, he was pro-devil . He said that in *Paradise Lost*, John Milton was of the devil's party without knowing it. These things are rather fluid. How the devil is functioning at a particular moment is more the point. Is it a devil that is going to open your life and bring you to new places? There is no necessary opposition between opposition and openness.

We talked about Rabbi Nachman not wanting to experience pleasure in sex. Some chassids would go to Rabbi Menachem Schneerson, leader of the Lubavitch group, and confess, "Rebbi, I masturbate. The evil impulse makes me do it." Schneerson tended to respond lightly about this. He thought it trivial compared to some of the problems humans face. Depending on the person, masturbation might be a little problem in the scheme of things, especially in comparison with more serious problems. It depends on how something is functioning in a situation. Good can be bad and bad can be good, depending on a particular context. In some contexts, masturbating can be a growth step, in others a barrier, in others business as usual.

Are you asking if I ever oppose a patient? Or oppose someone's oppositionalism? A devil opposing devils? Am I oppositional? You've had a dose of me today. You decide. I do lots of different things with patients, sometimes this, sometimes that. Often it just happens, a surprise. Although sometimes I assume whatever I do, whichever way I go, I'm probably wrong. An attitude I've learnt over the years is more freeing than feeling right.

Question 9:   I'm from Japan, but I don't know too much about Buddhism. But what you are talking about today is near to Zen Buddhism. [The tape lost several sentences of what was said.] Much is sensed by the body, not by language or thoughts. Western people try to understand by language and thoughts but Eastern people try to sense [again, something missed on tape] by the body itself.

Response 9:   Well, I'm not an expert in anything, but earlier I was talking about body sensation, so that might be a little close to what you are talking about. I was talking about body sensing and that there is even a God sensation as part of the background of our being. I am not a Zen master or anything like that, but I appreciate your speaking affirmatively about body feeling. I think a lot more is linked with body feeling than we are aware of. The term sense, too, spans many dimensions. It is a great unifying word, spanning body sensing, common sense and sense as meaning. If we had time, it would be worthwhile to have fuller discussion of this word "sense" and realities it touches.

Question 10:   In one of the NYU contemplative study groups, we are studying the *Satipatthana Sutta*, the first teaching the Buddha ever gave to the disciples. In it he teaches you to be mindful, starting with the breath. He speaks of the four abidings of mindfulness. The first is the body, the second the feelings, perceptions, the third is the mind, and the fourth insights of mind, such as emptiness, form is emptiness, emptiness is form, selflessness. So the body is one of the important things, but staying with mindfulness opens further possibilities of awareness. I think the word for mind in Buddhism is mind–body, mind–heart. It's a joined word, which I think you would enjoy because it doesn't separate those two words. So that the feelings that you have are completely in body and mind and include all of it and anything that arises and passes away. It is the object of the *sutra* to enable you slowly, by going through all the levels of the *sutra*, to be able to tolerate and suffer any state that arises, and not be impatient with it, not push it away, but just have the patience you have been talking about, and I really appreciate your putting it in very clinical and day to day terms.

Response 10:   Don't forget to include tolerance of our intolerance, since we can't take very much of anything really. But you can get the hang of that, too, not being able to tolerate too much—you dose it out.

Question 11:   In some of the emails and the Bion clip you sent there seemed to be some reference to joy, and I wondered if you could add a little to that.

Response 11:   During my meetings with Bion in New York, I remarked that I found him joyless. He quickly said, if joy is important to you, you have to embody it, it has to be in your skin. And then, at the very end of the seminar, Bion remarked on the pleasure, the joy, we get from psychoanalysis, and pleasure from going through the seminar together, the hard work we did. The joy of facing and going through difficulty, painful aspects of clinical work. He writes about suffering joy, building a more tolerant capacity to suffer experiencing, the experience of joy.

Question 12:   Why is beauty at the heart of the *Sephirot*? Pleasure and beauty have continually wafted through the realms of catastrophe in today's talk. Permit me to make one comment about beauty, in the text you cited the chassidic rabbi with whom I'm learning Torah. He says that Akiva came and went from the garden because of the four, he was complete, and what did this completeness mean? He enjoyed sex with his wife, so he could come and go. Another thing, it says in Genesis that the tree was pleasant to look at and good to eat. Pleasant to look at—here beauty came first.

Response 12:   Very nice. So, about Akiva, you remember that his wife put him up to being a *tzadik*. When they met he was ignorant, holy but illiterate. You know the story about Akiva as an illiterate child sitting in back of the *shul*. All he could say were words from the alphabet, *aleph, bet, gimel, dalet*—but he said them with all his heart. There was a glow in the back of the *shul* and the men would ask, "What's that glow?" The glow was above Akiva's head, growing from the strength of his *kavanna* (devotion, intensity, whole-heartedness).

When he met the woman who was to be his wife, he was still illiterate, and she said, "I'll marry you on the condition that you study Torah and become someone who knows." And so he did and became one of the great interpreters and seers. According to your rabbi, they had good sexual relations as well (although when he was studying, they were separated for long periods, but that might even have made it better). I was not going to speak much today on *Tiferet* (Beauty), the heart of the Tree of Life, but you have prompted me to say something. You told me that Akiva's glow was connected with sex with his wife—freely going in and out of the garden! Some of us know that glow well, probably many of us. But that does not explain Moses' glow. Moses stopped having sex with his wife when his spiritual journey started. Yet, when he returned to the children of Israel after being in the presence of YHVH, he was aglow. [He had] a glow of such magnitude that he wore a veil to shield the eyes of those who saw him. So there are glows and glows, an infinitude of dimensions of Beauty. "A thing of beauty is a joy forever", writes Keats. Contact with God gave Moses a glow he didn't get from his wife. I think, too, of Keats' "spirit ditties of no tone". Beauty radiates in all directions.

Tiferet, the centre of the *Sephirot*, which links them all together. It links all ten capacities or faculties, all levels, high–low, right–left, sexual–spiritual. How beautiful the mother must look to the baby—in one of their moods, at certain moments—a look that remains at the centre of the soul, a sense of beauty waiting to be aroused. The mother can look like a witch or be a bringer of beautiful feelings, depending on the mood of the moment. A beauty that carries over into erotic beauty, into transcendental beauty. In a way, you could say beauty unites the body. Think of the ancient Greek emphasis on beauty in the harmony of capacities.

Beauty has a bigger meaning than we tend to give it in this country. We come close to it when we talk about someone who has a beautiful soul. But we know from literature, and literature knows from life and vision, that there can be an intimate and tragic link between beauty and destruction. Melville's Billy Budd, a beautiful soul, an innocent, becomes a murderer when confronted by mendacious authority. Again, the beautiful ideals of the French Revolution followed by slaughter, a conjunction that history repeats (Arendt, 1970, 2006). Or the conjunction of beauty and destruction at the beginning of the Western canon, the erotic theft that begins the Trojan wars in Homer's *Iliad*. A conjunction with frequent consequences in everyday life. Beauty can function in a creative, life-giving way or in a destructive way. We are made up of double-edged, multi-edged processes. How something functions in particular contexts changes values. Perhaps in another seminar we can say more about why beauty is the heart of the tree of life, the tree of faith. Why faith is beautiful.

CHAPTER TWO

The second seminar

I t's been a wild few weeks here—a hurricane, a nor'easter, a presidential election. So much damage, so much hope. How many people here saw Obama's last or near last campaign speech where he repeatedly says, "Are you fired up?" Three people? There won't be too much of a response then, but we'll try.

"Are you fired up?"
"Ready to go!" [a few people said, more whisper than shout.]
You're supposed to say, "Ready to go!" Let's try it again.
"Are you fired up? Are you fired up?!" [laughter]
"Ready to go!" [this time a good outcry from the room]

All right! Obama told a story about hearing this cry from a woman in a small town he visited. He showed up for a campaign meeting with about twenty people present. While he waited, he kept hearing a sound, at first in the background, then louder and louder. A lady was saying, "Are you fired up?" Then someone would say, "Ready to go!" The cry mounted. A small group of loyal campaigners lifting spirit.

The Kabbalah has passages about creating reality with words. During the presidential campaign, I would feel how one side or another would try to shape reality with words. There were times when alternating views of reality seemed invincible. There are moments you lose track that these are just people making up things, trying to convince you of one position or another. Yet, things you make up have consequences. Like the group that kept insisting that Saddam Hussein had weapons of mass destruction and was a threat to our country. Many people were killed and maimed as a consequence of such a vision (Eigen, 2006b).

There's a piece in the Kabbalah about Joseph's dream in which his brothers bow down to him. Naturally, his brothers were angry at such grandiosity and sought to do Joseph harm. Twenty-two years later, in Egypt, they do bow down to him. Yet, the Kabbalah says, had they interpreted the dream differently and had a different response, something else might have happened. Had they gone deeper and experienced the divine nature in themselves, another world of experience could have appeared. Perhaps the story gives us a choice between arrogance and devotion or, better, encourages us to learn how to interact with both of these sides of our nature in better ways.

It's all right to be sceptical, an important part of our nature. A critical mind can be spirited by a devotional element. You could say the story shows how nasty we can be and often are with each other. How mixed reality is. How mysterious its turns. You can bring out how our attitudes boomerang, reverse. Critical and devotional attitudes need cultivating. They are like brothers that have their own growth trajectories. In the Bible, brothers are often at odds. This can be seeing life as it is in such cases. But, as a psychologist, I have to add another dimension as well, an inner one, and see such stories as portrayals of dual attitudes within ourselves. Dual attitudes that can be antagonistic, at war, or friendly at times, even fused, symbiotic, co-nurturing. How to make room for them both, and allow for more partnership?

*   *   *

As is a tradition in the NYU Contemplative Studies Project, we will start with a little guided meditation. So, I invite you to be calm, relax, quiet, feel your own quietness. It says in the Bible that wisdom begins with quietness and this little meditation will be on wisdom, love of wisdom, wisdom of love.

[Spoken slowly, with many pauses]

Chochma, Wisdom, the Second *Sephira*

Relax your body, your soul . . .

Let my words wash over you, through you . . .

No need to force

No need to worry

There is no wrong now . . . For this moment, you can't do anything wrong

Chochma

Wisdom

Love of Wisdom

Wisdom of Love

Wisdom lives in you

You are wisdom

Wisdom is in your cells, in your pores

All through you

You are skin wisdom, heart wisdom, head and gut wisdom,

Wisdom in your glands

You are sexual wisdom, breath wisdom

Ears are wisdom, eyes are wisdom, tongue is wisdom

All of you bathed in wisdom

Wisdom in your tears, in your kindness, in your strength,

In your hate, your meanness,

You sense it, it tastes you

It finds the secret places you need

Secret places waiting to be touched

At last wisdom finds them

At last wisdom finds you

You and your wisdom sit quietly with each other

Wisdom and you together

Sitting quietly a little while . . .

*　*　*

Before the Tree of Life, the *sephirot*, there was—who knows?—it is called so many names: nothing, infinity, emptiness, some words are used like "not" or "that" or "what." One name you know is *Ein Sof*, without bounds, no limit, no name, no conception, no imagining, yet we somehow feel it. We have a special sense organ somewhere that feels it, that senses it. I don't know whether all of us do, I do not have that knowledge, but I know that many of us do. We sense this name-less, wordless, imageless, conception-less presence and parts of the Kabbalah call it the mystery within the mystery, or the concealed within the concealed, or the secret within the secret.

It is described as changeless, yet also as developing, becoming manifest, unconcealed, emergent, revealed, while still concealed, unmanifest. No amount of emanation, manifestation, exhausts its secret. I think of W. R. Bion talking about embryonic or beginning-less no-place, no-thing. At the same time the Kabbalah describes it as luminous, so dark it shines. I love Hindu descriptions of The Great Light. The *Zohar* speaks of a High Spark in all the sparks that grow, that emanate from it.

Kabbalah is fantasy, perhaps more deeply, dream. Religion is fantasy about what is intimated, You cannot put it down on an insurance form. You cannot say something is happening but I don't know what or how. Yet, it does something to you. What can one say? If you call it emptiness, it fills your life. Chuang Tzu says, "I know there's a master builder somewhere but I don't know where or how or what. The Creator has identity but no form."

So, before the *sephirot* there was endless, we don't have words for it, endless dimensions of "not" or infinite, infinitudes of infinity. Bion calls the fundamental psychic reality infinite, that no religion or art can come anywhere near describing. An experience of paradoxical mystery. The *sephirot* emanate from this unknown primary dimension. A reality that remains unknown as it reveals itself through the *sephirot* and other manifestations. The *sephirot* are expressions of what cannot be captured. We are expressive beings and part of our expressiveness touches, mediates invisible sensing that eludes meanings we give it. If one literalises the *sephirot* or literalises Bion's grid (Image 2, p. 9) or Kundalini *chakras*, one misses living reality. Bion writes that he can evoke an experience he has with a patient but cannot represent it. We can give expression to what we sense without being satisfied by ways we express it.

At the top of the *sephirot* is the crown *sephira* called *Keter*, which has commonalities with the crown *chakra* in Kundalini yoga. It is a "first" emanation from the Unmanifest. In the *chakra* system, an opening to infinity. An opening to a spiritual world beyond everything we know, yet implicit in what we know. It can manifest in many ways. Peace beyond peace, bliss beyond bliss. Perfect mercy, akin to the Buddhist *Kwan Yin*.

In one diagram I saw, the gap between *Keter* and *Ein Sof* was called the abyss. In some others, various phases of unmanifest and manifest Light. By the time we get to *Keter*, we have travelled a long way—a lot goes on before we get to *Keter*. A parallel in Bion is all the unknown, unmanifest transformations that go on before we get to the grid, all the unconscious work underlying emergence of beta and alpha elements. One reason these formulations are magical has to do with their attempts to express something sensed beyond expression. Unseen, unheard "bees of the invisible", to play with Rilke. Or Keats: "spirit ditties of no tone".

A lot goes on off the grid. A lot goes on before we get to the *sephirot*. A lot goes on between and within the categories of the grid that we do not have names for. A lot goes on between and within the *sephirot* that we lack names for. One mode of expression human beings have used to touch related realms of experience involves the duality: eternity and time, myriad eternal and temporal worlds, dimensions. We search for a language of the ineffable.

In some of Bion's descriptions one feels outside of time, no-time and time at the same time. He depicts, for example, a catastrophic explosion at the origins (O) of personality with bits of personality flying away from each other and their point of origin at accelerating velocity (Bion, 1970; Eigen, 1998). Bion accesses some of these flying bits of personality from a temporal perspective but often they come from—or seem to come from—spaces that defy time.

The grid traps the untrappable and, therefore, fails. The *sephirot* mediate the unknowable and, therefore, fail. Yet, both succeed in expressing something, in seeking something. We are, I think, partly talking about nuances of states, for example, fusions and antagonisms between no-time and time states, both of which have variations. Bion, for example, describes an analysis as one moment extended in space–time. He seeks to give expression to that moment or moments, aware that it is his special physical–social–psychical–spiritual apparatus mediating it.

Bion's image of analysis as the unfolding of a moment reminds me of a well-known Einstein quote:

> A human being is a part of the whole called by us universe, a part limited in time and space. He experiences himself, his thoughts and feeling as something separated from the rest, a kind of optical delusion of his consciousness. This delusion is a kind of prison for us, restricting us to our personal desires and to affection for a few persons nearest to us. Our task must be to free ourselves from this prison by widening our circle of compassion to embrace all living creatures and the whole of nature in its beauty. (Einstein, 1950)

Other associations: the heart *sutra*'s emphasis on going beyond beyond; the illusion Chassidism calls the concatenation, or the *Zohar* calls assemblages, or Chuang Tzu calls bells and whistles. Or a song my mother would sing to me, "merrily, merrily down the stream, life is but a dream".

In our first seminar almost three years ago (Eigen, 2012a), I pointed out that the Kabbalah is a kind of archipelago of many works, lots of moments of meditation many people had, many not written down but passed on orally. How far back in time is disputed. Authorship of even the most influential works is disputed. There are groups today that claim the *Zohar*, an especially important landmark, was authored by Shimon bar Yohai in the first century; scholars found it was authored by Moshe de Leon in thirteenth century Spain. More recently, it is thought a number of authors in addition to Moshe de Leon contributed tracts that were pasted together, although he remains the main author. Basic experiences and ideas get renewed and reinterpreted as transformational processes continue. Experiential threads keep developing with a certain fluidity rather than fixed dogma.

The *Sefer Yezirah*, sometimes said to be the earliest or among the earliest of Kabbalah texts, was said to contain visions received by Abraham. Some thought it written two hundred years BCE, some thought it written two hundreds years CE. Some say it was perhaps a twelfth century text. It depicted ten *sephirot*, but over time there have been differences as to what the ten might be and how they function. There is no settled agreement as to authorship or when it was written. Yet, generation after generation of people who study Kabbalah tracts, whatever their uncertainties, gain inspiration, vision, and are enriched by possibilities of experience and reflection.

Some kabbalists felt *Keter* (crown) so close to the supernal realm that it was not truly a *sephira* but above them, part of the heavenly realms. Some began the tree with the second *sephira*, *Chochma*, wisdom, and added *Daat*, knowledge, as the third (*Chochma, Binah, Daat: Chabad*, a signature of the Lubavitch Chassidim.). *Daat*—a very special knowing, direct knowing of the divine. To keep both *Keter* and *Daat* in the Tree of Life, in time *Keter* was put back on top, *sephira* number one, and *Daat* was put in parenthesis, not officially a *sephira*, but a capacity plugged into the divine, roughly represented in what approximates the throat *chakra*, joining head, and body with the divine. Some associate it with the middle, or third, eye, emphasising its profound perception of the divine. All *sephirot* have linking capacities, including links with each other in endless ways.

Now, let me talk a little more about *Keter*, since it is the top-most *sephira*, the start of the tree, part of the "first" emanation that begins the *sephirot*, with ambiguity as to whether it is part of the heavenly realm and/or a special link or conduit of godly energy initiating and informing the *sephirot*.

Keter has an outer and inner aspect. An outer manifestation is will, divine will, intention. Its inner dimensions have various names, including faith and humility. Sometimes it is depicted as pure good, unmixed loving kindness, as upper-upper realms are transmitted, transmuted through *Keter*. It is so pure, so near to and one with purity that it is represented as a long face, an extended countenance, a face so large it touches, goes through, and links all the other *sephirot*. Two of its names are Arik Anpin and Macroprosopus. It has only a right side, no left, and is depicted as a white skull. One of the things that I feel critical of in the Kabbalah, and religion in general, is over-emphasis on one or another capacity. Here, a drive towards purity.

As a psychologist, I cannot help feeling our drive for purity is rooted, partly, in how bad we feel. This, I realise, coheres with much religious thought. One aspect of religion has to do with purifying ourselves from sinful thoughts, impulses, deeds. A sense of evil or something amiss runs deep (Eigen, 1999). The Kabbalah is guilty of this, too, but it has potential to rectify itself. It emphasises balance, interaction of capacities, in fertile ways. When caught in extremes, it can emphasise creative imbalance. It is rooted in a creative view of the universe and life.

The notion that the purity of Arik Anpin/Macroprosopus, extends through the whole tree gives ground for faith or hope; a sense that some degree or point of purity remains no matter where we find ourselves. That Grace exists and can reach and transform us anywhere, anytime, as we are, this moment.

As we descend the tree, another, smaller face emerges. The emotional or middle *sephirot*, Zeir Anpin, Microprosopus, "Lesser Countenance". These include the fourth *sephira*, *Chesed* (mercy, loving kindness), the fifth, *Gevurah* (strength, judgement, severity), the sixth, *Tiferet* (beauty), seventh, *Netzach* (endurance, persistence), eighth, *Hod* (flexibility, plasticity, openness), and the ninth, *Yesod* (foundation, fecundity, genitals).

According to this scheme, the Long Face (intellect, intuition) dominates and organises Small Face (emotions, passions), although the latter inform and enrich the former. This accords with Plato and Aristotle's hierarchy of capacities, which has suffered doubt with the persistence of destructiveness in human life.

In Kabbalah, the divine flow goes from top down, as capacities needed to create and sustain the world emerge. Once these structural processes are in place, the flow between them can go in any direction, since all *sephirot* are complexly connected (and, in my view, unexpected connections continue to grow). As above, so below, as below, so above is one formula expressing multi-directionality of possibilities. It can be enriching to sit down and try to diagram possible interactions between capacities, states, tendencies expressed by the *sephirot*. You could not exhaust them. More keep emerging. Creative possibilities are endless.

One image, perhaps a variation of foetal development, depicts a skull on top of the tree from which marvellous dew drips down, a dew of light which begins to illuminate and bring to life further capacities below (Mathers, 1887). We can locate this luminous, birthing, dew-dripping skull with *Keter*, either at the beginning of the tree or an in-between land, an emanation of the supernal realm. The dew is a prototype of the manna that fed the Israelites in the desert. A dew that sustains and pro-creates, creating a second face, a face of emotional life, with special connection to *Tiferet* (beauty), the heart of the Kabbalah tree.

There are rough correspondences between the *sephirot* and the human body. *Keter* with the crown of the head, *Chochma* and *Binah* with the right and left brain, *Daat* with the throat. *Chesed* with the right arm, *Gevurah* with the left arm, *Tiferet* with the heart, *Netzach* with the right hip, leg, *Hod* with the left, *Yesod* with genitals, *Malchut* with feet. *Chochmah* and *Binah* can unite as "third eye" in Kundalini yoga. *Daat* can unite throat and third eye in a direct pipeline to divinity. *Tiferet* has correspondences to the heart *chakra*. Interweaving is inexhaustible.

The Kabbalah tree is one of the greatest spiritual light shows you can find, filled with nothingness and luminous fireworks. It seems to take on life of its own, drenched in fecundity. I have sometimes seen it represented by neural networks generating new patterns. Biologists have adapted it to depict the evolution of life. The image of a tree, whether used to depict spiritual or biological networks, tends to be hierarchical, with emphasis on upper–lower (perceptual dimensions a tree and human body have in common), with the limitations that vertical hierarchical vision brings (Eigen, 1986, Chapter Six).

Near the end of the *Zohar*, Rabbi Shimon tells us that his mouth cannot stop singing. This is one of many expressions of the creativity theme that permeates so much of the Kabbalah. The Rabbi Shimon part of us, a faith part of us, life-faith, cannot stop singing. From this place, we can picture the Unmanifest Unknown singing the *sephirot* and existence into being. Mixtures of joy and catastrophe, a primacy of joy. King David, through all the horrors of life and descents of the soul depicted in his songs, ends with drums and horns, dancing, singing, strumming, blowing, making music. He dedicates his song to the Great Musician.

There are varied stories of beginnings. I wrote of Macro- and Microprosopos. I could have chosen others. Rabbi Shimon tells us there is no end to beginnings, no end to inspiration (in-spirit), the fountains keep flowing. The *sephirot* tree is something like a spiritual kaleidoscope. Turn it this way, that, more patterns and colours configure. There are various names of God associated with each *sephira*. Singing and naming. One cannot exhaust the Nameless.

Another name for higher reaches of the nameless is the holy ancient of ancient ones. By the time it reaches *Keter* it is called *Ayeh Asher Ayeh*: I will be there, I am. By the time this force reaches *Tiferet* it is called the blessed one. Depending on who is writing, *Tiferet* is associated with YHVH (the God force that creates the world and its rules), Jacob, William Blake's Jesus as Divine Imagination. Imagination, perhaps, because we wonder, could anyone think up a world like this? Bion suggests asking ourselves when we see a patient, could we have imagined someone just like this existing before we met? If we are honest, we have to say, no, I could not have. Each of us is a revelation, a new song.

There are many resonances through the ages. *Keter's* "I will be there" gets inverted by Freud to where id (It) is, I will be, which Lacan amplifies to I will go where It goes. I will follow wherever it leads. Like Freud letting the horse (the unconscious) lead the way, the "I" following. Reminiscent of Ruth telling Naomi, "Where you go, I will go." A structure that overlaps with the ten Zen ox-herding pictures by Shuben (fifteenth century). A young man spots prints that he follows into the forest, following the unknown where it leads, until the ox (unconscious life, the vast mind, the universe) is spotted and one begins the effort to ride it, to the point of effortlessly letting the ox lead the way towards enlightenment (Milner, 1987).

One might say *Keter's* I will be there suggests the beginning of time, the God of temporality, *yesh* (being)—if time can have a beginning. Another name for some early, pre-*sephirot*, supernal realms is *ayin*, nothing. Another "pre-time" name is *Ein (Ayin) Sof*, no end, no limit, without boundaries. Another pre-time domain, before, or higher than, the *sephirot*, is *Ein Sof Or*, limitless light (overlapping with The Great Light of Hindu teachings). Perhaps we can come back to these dimensions later. For now, I would just like to make a notation and put a double arrow between being and nothingness, *ayin* and *yesh*: *ayin* ↔ *yesh*, and suggest that we have a double capacity that nulls and affirms, zeros and creates. A domain where nulling and creation go together.

*   *   *

The trickling down of divine dew and Light initiating emergent capacities is one image. Sixteenth-century Lurianic Kabbalah emphasises another. The sheer immensity and force of unmediated Godly energy was too much for emergent capacities meant to mediate it and some of the *sephirot* shattered as they were created. Vehicles of creation could not take the intensity of the creative force. Just as we, Bion suggests, are challenged by our own affective intensity. Sometimes I say, rather dramatically, that God could not take his own intensity and partly broke under the strain of his being. One breaks under the strain of being oneself.

There is the image, too, that God's name breaks apart, partly because of God's self-impact and partly because of our negative impacts on ourselves, on the universe, on God. A good deal of energy in Jewish mysticism goes into putting God's name back together. There are double references in prayer to a time when God's name is One, is One now, and through efforts of prayer and repair will be One once again in the future. From this vertex, we play a role in repairing a tear in God.

Some readings say the upper *sephirot* break and by the time Godly energy reaches the lower *sephirot*, it is diminished and more tolerable. Other readings say the upper *sephirot* remain a part of God, while the lower ones break. The greater distance from the supernal, the more broken. The last *sephirot*, the tenth, *Malchut* (Figure 1, p. 3), our time–space material world, is the most broken of all. One of our jobs here is perpetual repair.

There is a special link between the first *sephira*, *Keter*, and the last, *Malchut*. I mentioned an inner dimension of *Keter*, the *sephira* closest to the supernal realm (a direct emanation of it), is faith. And faith is a crucial element in *Malchut*, the realm of earthly action, as well. A direct link between the faith of *Keter* and faith of *Malchut*, between the highest and lowest, a two way stream. One speaks of the *Keter* in *Malchut* and the *Malchut* in *Keter*, a union of spirit–mind–feeling–body. Head in feet, feet in head. In effect, all the *sephirot* are in all the others, like yin in yang and yang in yin. A complex, unending interweaving of capacities and functions.

It is said the right side is male, the left side is female. Although this does not hold up exactly, you get a lot of meditative punch from it. The most explicit female *sephira* is *Binah*, understanding, the mother. *Chochma*, wisdom, the father, links with *Binah*, who gives birth to the *sephirot* below her. *Chochma* is created from the *yud* (j), the first letter of YHVH. The *yud* looks like semen, tear, and flame. *Binah* is created from the *hay* (h), the second letter of YHVH (read from right to left:

hvhj), which looks like a house, ear, or container with an opening. The *sephirot* flow from the name of God in a special way through *Binah*, the mother. The tenth and last *sephira, Malchut,* our realm of earthly action and pursuits, is associated with the *Shechinah*, carrier of faith, God's feminine side, daughter of *Binah*. The inner life of the bottom through the inner life of the top, united by faith. Faith as a stream through the inner life of the *sephirot*.

The Kabbalah tree, the *Sephirot*, is often called the Tree of Life and is also called the Tree of Faith. In some commentaries, Faith is called the biggest tree in the garden. By faith, I do not mean belief. One can fight over systems of belief. But faith is something deeper than the contents of belief, deeper than fighting. Part of a stream that waters and gives rise to religious impulse but cannot be reduced to the latter. A profound sense of faith can grow without being exhausted by definitions.

I think therapy has a lot to do with faith. So many sessions are dramas of faith, crises of faith. Some feelings involved might have to do with whether or not life is worth living. This is not just a mental debate, but a feeling that affects one's being, one's inner taste of life. There are ways that life hangs in the balance, as one swings between a sense that life is worth living and is not. The mood or spirit of a session might hover between life and death (Eigen, 1996, 1999).

A kind of every day faith is part of daily life, part of getting up in the morning and doing all that a day asks one to do. Unexpected happenings can affect one's faith barometer, sending it into tailspins, keeping it level, lifting it higher. One can move between moments of grace and emotional hits that send one reeling, not only knocking the breath out, but threatening to do one in for a time. A lot of drama goes on in rhythms of recovery. In extreme moments, one finds oneself wavering between faith and loss of faith in living. Loss of faith, too, if one opens to it, can lead to new discoveries.

*   *   *

In the *Zohar*, I find an intimate connection between a sense of goodness and faith. Plato's Idea of the Good is at the top of his hierarchy, the form of forms, that which underlies the working of spiritual reality, the highest pinnacle of apprehension and, perhaps, the unconscious foundation of essence and existence. Near the beginning of the Bible, God appreciates his creative activity and says it is good.

Near the beginning of the *Zohar* there are images, phrases, and stories suggesting that whatever goodness exists in the world keeps it going. Without goodness there could be no world. If goodness vanished, the world would vanish. An association of faith and goodness touches the question, is this life worth living, is this life good enough to live? Is part of faith, faith in goodness? Is it an inherent part of goodness?

Most of us have heard the phrase, faith in living, but its potential counterpart, faith in dying or beyond dying is not as common. When Job says even if you slay me I will trust You, is this faith beyond all usual content? Faith without a reference? We speak of natural faith, blind faith, spiritual faith. Perhaps a shared sense runs through them, without being able to pin down what or where it is. In common sense, everyday parlance, does it have to do with a way aliveness feels now? This moment but also under this moment, beyond this moment, a Moment of moments, a faith feeling, sensation, affective attitude. Something living in *Malchut* distils, heightens by challenging it, heightens by doing it in. There are ways, I fear, that faith can grow by being ripped apart. Faith that strengthens by being nulled, that takes us to unanticipated places when there is no cause for it to exist at all.

* * *

My favourite *sephira* is *Tiferet*, Beauty (Figure 1, p. 3). The uplifting quality of beauty, the inspiration of beauty, the faith of beauty. Keats: a thing of beauty is a joy forever. So many kinds of beauty. It is associated with compassion, harmony, heart. Yet, one of its God names is YHVH, the blessed holy one, the smaller countenance. The Nameless, Unrepresentable, Unimaginable with a history of breaking apart and restoration, reward–punishment, exile and return, expressed through Jacob and Moses.

Perhaps the God level expressed by YHVH helps to keep the brakes on beauty. Beauty by itself can take us beyond good and evil, right and wrong, true and false. Beauty for its own sake, and how it fills and lifts us. A beautiful moment touches us whether we are good or bad, deserving or not. A moment of beauty is its own reward. It gives us reprieve from the binaries, using or even dissolving the latter in service of greater harmony.

Jacob marrying Leah represents living on the level of law and custom. Jacob marrying Rachel represents the opening of the heart.

Like Mary and Martha, they express different states of mind and soul, both of which we live by, different qualities of practicality and devotion. To reflect on the ten *sephirot* and what is beyond them makes us more aware and appreciative of interplay and dissociations between capacities that make us up, that enliven existence.

Any of the *sephirot* can work in a negative or positive way, depending on use, function, attitude. *Gevurah*, for example represents strength and discrimination or judgement. We need to evaluate, to experience differences and create hypotheses that lead to action. Perception gives us the world as organised in various ways, forms, colour, relations between objects and events, varying fields of experience. We tell the difference between this and that in order to move from here to there. Yet judgement can spiral and become severe. Psychoanalysis points out that what it calls "superego" represents ethical concerns but can take a negative turn, spiral out of contact with reality, become over-condemning. One can become hyper-critical of human failings, one's own and others, to the extent that one becomes semi-paralysed or chronically enraged. We are gifted with so many capacities that keeping a balance is ever challenging. It is so easy to get caught between self-indulgence and self-condemnation, twin tendencies.

In many cases, I have seen a strong need to condemn human flaws to be a kind of self-indulgence with addictive qualities. Severe judgement as an addiction. A well-known Jewish tale shows that even saints can share such a weakness. Rabbi Shimon bar Yohai, first century *tzadik* (righteous one, wise one), was said to hide in a cave for twelve years with his son, Eliezar, also a great *tzadik*. While hiding from the Romans, they studied the holy book and it is said Rabbi Shimon wrote or orally transmitted the seeds of the *Zohar*, the most influential of Jewish mystical texts (see above, p. 52). After twelve years, they learnt of a change in Roman government or attitude, and thought it safe enough to return. But when they were again among their people, their eyes, having grown accustomed to the most holy, mystical experience, burned through the flesh and souls of ordinary people. One might express this hyperbolically, saying their look caused others to disintegrate on the spot. Seeing this, God told them, "You spent twelve years alone with me and this is how you treat my people? Back to your cave for twelve more years!" Some say twelve months was enough and they returned with appreciative loving kindness (from the negative aspect of *Gevurah* to the positive aspect of *Tiferet*).

Some even say that the origin of evil is in the negative aspect of *Gevurah*, judgement gone wild, like a cancer, proliferating severity and fear. Bion describes this as a mad part of personality and in some passages calls it "ego-destructive superego". By ego-destructive he means a tendency to destroy independent, critical thinking and growth. Or, simply, destruction of a fuller capacity to experience the waves of life. He is a spokesperson for remaining open to development of complexity and multiplicity, with emphasis on caring use of attention (a capacity perhaps taken for granted, not receiving the full attention it deserves in Kabbalah journeys, although it is present implicitly).

Bion writes of difficulties we have in tolerating the build up of experience. Often we break off as an experience begins to build. So many dreams are about aborted feeling, feeling that is too scary or too much for us in some way and we wake up before a feeling can run to its conclusion. Often we represent intensity in dreams by figures that attack us (Eigen, 2005). Attacked by feeling we cannot endure. Freud's formulation of drives exerting force on personality touches a similar problem. Often, we are deformed by drive pressures, pushes and pulls we do not seem able to handle. Freud suggests that at times these pressures can lead to permanent deformation of personality. We are pressured by our own personality, unable to tolerate ourselves, persecuted by aspects of our being. Like the breaking of the vessels meant to mediate God's creative energy, we can be traumatised by our own intensity, our own makeup. Persecuted by our own being, human nature, our energy and multiplicity or, in Freud's formulation, by our drives. What do we do with our drives? Channel them? Become more neurotic, psychotic, or psychopathic? Will we always be, to some extent, driven beings?

What to do with our drivenness? There are, too, parallels between drive and will. Often what we call "will" drives us, pushes us in this or that direction. We can sometimes say that will pushes us against our will. Saint Paul touched this when he said that things he would do, he doesn't and things he doesn't want to do, he does. Will, like Eros, can have a will of its own. We can be swept along by a powerful burst or push of will against our better interests.

Kabbalah depicts an external aspect of *Keter*, the first and top-most *sephira*, as divine will, a will that permeates the *sephirot* below it. Let us suppose that it is a positive will, suffused with loving, creative intention. Lurianic Kabbalah tells us that even this most positive will can be too much for systems that must support it. The very channels that are to mediate divine will break under the charge. Repair of brokenness becomes a major human challenge. Can one repair damaged channels of transmission by damaged capacities, damaged by the force of positive divine will itself? It is an ancient theme that human beings cannot see God directly and live. Filter systems are necessary. But even the filter systems are in jeopardy, might not be up to the task. A human situation: to repair brokenness with brokenness. It would seem a call for compassion and mutual support rather than condemnation. Perhaps the surplus of condemnation becomes, partly, a measure of the brokenness it condemns and exacerbates.

Faith, the inner life of *Keter*, contrasts with the force of will and perhaps even intention. A lovely moment is Matthew 6:28, the passage on the lilies of the field, how they grow, not toiling or spinning, growing spontaneously according to their own nature as God nurtures them. In our life, faith associated with grace and love, not a matter of willpower and control, but a free happening. A moment of freedom. Not "free-will" but a moment free of will.

In real life, there are endless permutations of faith and will, sometimes more one or the other. Various mixtures, faith in will, will in faith. Still, a moment of freedom from will is a reference point of one's existence. A breath of fresh air, life freely breathing. A moment of being free from the pressure of oneself.

When we come back to our driven selves, we wonder what can we do with our drivenness. At times, it leads us to new heights, possibilities of creation, learning, building. At times, it rips us apart, brings us to our knees, drills unforgiving holes in all we have built. At times, we try to manage these two parts of our nature, a dialectic of faith and will, by envisioning a reward-and-punishment God. Rewarding us with good if only we are good enough. At times, this God falls apart and we are taken beyond any system of merits to a raw reality impossible to envision. At such a juncture, some of us report dying over and over, death as a living reality—living death. Falling into an endless meat grinder, grinding our inner beings into paste, formlessness. Such a moment becomes a repeated happening, part of our lives. We might look forward to it, ridding us of our built up selves, leading to another kind of freedom, an illusion of starting from scratch. Or, perhaps, a sense of empty spaces within the network of our selves, our personality, interstices where grace can enter, a welcome wind blowing through chambers of our being. I think of one of Flannery O'Connor's "pious" characters, the surprise on her face, when, after dying, even her virtues are burnt away. There is a dimension better than reward and punishment. Moments that take us past knots and twists that oppress.

In everyday language, we speak of good will and evil will, good and evil imagination. Our emotions vibrate immediately to the variable combinations. Yahweh is perhaps one of the most formidable representations of this ambivalent mixture, since all good and evil come from Him. There is deep wisdom in representing the outer dimension of *Keter* as will, the inner as faith. Two sides of God's personality, our personality. Colours on the palette of our soul, our experience. Experience that presses for more experience and as it presses, more beckons, opens. Creative circles interlocking with destructive circles, seeming to separate and go different ways, fusing again. Evil will, good will, all the concatenations. And a whisper of something else, life deeper than these circles, beyond the noose.

The *Sephirot*, as we study them today, are largely canonical, more set than they once might have been. Even now, there is much fluidity, layers of meaning, shifts. It may be hard to imagine that in some systems the fifth *sephira*, now called *Gevurah*, may once have been Life rather than Strength. *Gevurah* is associated with the God name *Elohim*, associated with judgement, with a tendency to veer towards becoming what psychoanalysis calls a severe superego, overly strict, condemning. If we focus on this one transformation, we might glimpse a tendency in Life to over-organise itself, a developmental trajectory towards more constriction–restriction. It leaves its residue in the sixth *sephira*, *Tiferet*, meant to balance, harmonise, synthesise *sephira* four (mercy) and five (judgement), one reason the God name for *Tiferet* often is YHVH, who represents both capacities in His reward–punishment aspect, while retaining His status as beyond imagining, inconceivable, unknowable, un-nameable.

What seem to be rigid categories (the *sephirot*) turn out to be fluid seas, with mutually transforming capacities. If you have a problem, particularly an unsolvable, relentless one, I recommend placing it (like a note in the Temple wall) into the sephirotic machine, press the on button and let it go to work. It may masticate, grind the knot to smithereens, dissolve it, restore it, change it. Whatever the result, there is a good chance you will not feel the same.

One can glean from the scheme of the *sephirot* that something is always beginning. The *sephirot* themselves are presented as emergent capacities. Emergence here takes on complex multi-directional meaning. One can say, each *sephira* emerges from the preceding one. At the same time, all are interdependent and each contains all the others. No matter where we start, if we look close enough, more and more capacities emerge. Beginning never ceases.

This coheres with a structure that defines the Bible. Creation never ceases. The Bible begins with creation and the many stories and happenings that ensue can be looked at as the fate or vicissitudes of creative acts. Stories of creativity, the drama of creativity, creative dramas. We are here in the midst of human narrative about Divine action and our relation to the Divine. If we take what we try to signal by the word God seriously, there is no beginning, Creativity always "was". There is nothing but creativity, always. Our narratives are handles, hands pointing, touching, seeking to find and define and evoke.

Kabbalists, like many other mystics, at a loss for expression, speak of infinities, *ayin* ("nothing") as "preceding" the time of worldly creation, our world. In the *Sephirot*, *ayin* tends to be most intimately linked with *Keter*, the *sephira* closest to the supernal, a first emanation. But it informs all the *sephirot*, interlaces existence, *yesh* (being). Infinities of *ayin* everywhere always. Visionary postulations of unknowable beginningless–endless dimensions surrounding–permeating existence, supporting our lives. The "highest" realms are beyond conflict, often envisioned as pure Mercy or Love, beyond or pre-opposites that, from our point of view, are transcended. But from on high there is nothing to transcend.

It seems fittingly accurate to call the God who creates our world *Elohim*, the God of *Gevurah*, and later, YHVH, God of conflict and choice, the drive for harmony and balance, yet still the un-nameable.

The first words of Genesis: *Berashis borah Elohim. Berashis*—in or with the beginning. *Borah*—creating, created. *Elohim*, the God of discrimination, judgement and, in its spiralling form, severity. A God of conflict, reward, and punishment. Creator of a domain requiring human struggle on many planes, including struggle with oneself, one's inner as well as outer environment. We have reached a level of Godhood that requires a God who can put the brakes on, tell the difference between this and that, create what some refer to as the concatenation, assemblage, or, as Chuang Tzu calls it, the "bells and whistles" of creation, forests of created–creating beings. "Whistles" partly refers to the hollows through which wind blows, creating breath and sound, *"ruach Elohim"*, God's breath.

Elohim is the God-name used at the beginning of Genesis to tell a creation story. *Elohim* is God-name in a feminine plural form. Many think it an androgynous god, male–female who created an androgynous being, Adam. For example, Mathers (1887) brings out the importance of the feminine plural form of *Elohim* and reacts strongly against redactors cleaning up God's name, making it solely male ("and they were religious men!" he says).

The name *Elohim* is repeated perhaps ten times in the first sentences of the Bible, in which the world, its creatures, the first humans and the Sabbath are created, the seven days of creation. *Elohim* as the God-name lets us know from the beginning that our world is one of conflict and struggle, labour and suffering—but not only. The Garden remains within us, too, and one mystical name for our world, at the level of *Malchut*, is Orchard. There is a Chassidic saying, that the world stands in the balance, a scale evenly balanced between good and evil, and any good deed, thought, word at any time can tip the scale towards the good and bring immediate redemption to the whole world. That is, move creation from the plane of struggle to the plane of Grace. In our life here and now, Grace interlaces struggle. But in the world to come, which can be any moment, life will be lived in Grace.

As a psychologist, I tend to see the two planes described as two attitudes, moments, states. A shift of attitude can bring one closer to one or the other. There is always a possibility that, for a time at least, one can rise above the storm, find a place of reprieve above or below the turbulence. Unmerited (outside the world of merits and demerits), amazing grace, just so.

*   *   *

Since I was a boy, I wondered about the first three words of the Bible and its inverted meaning, "In the beginning created God". When I came into more explicit contact with mystical Judaism, I found this to be a debated topic, with much passionate commentary. The God of Gods, so to speak, the ineffable *Ein Sof* of the nameless infinities was not named as the creator of our world. The God manifestation *Elohim* was, a God aspect perhaps, a form or function of God, God in one of his abilities. The God of judgement was created by In the Beginning. The Beginningless beginning birthed the God function necessary for the emergence of our world, a realm of differentiation, struggle, and conflict, involving good and evil and life and death. "In the Beginning" is a key here. I take it, in part, to mean "In the beginning" is always happening, always a reality, a resource. We share in this quality of beginning. In one of its forms, Bion calls it our embryonic capacity, Berdyaev speaks of neonic (neo-natal) freedom, Tao speaks of the unformed, Buddhism points to the uncreated, unborn, unoriginated.

We emerged from and are part of "in the beginning" which never stops. In the beginning is always part of us. Namelessness is always part of us, in our world connected with possibility, something further happening. In fact, we cannot exhaust our experience of namelessness, linked with radical openness. Namelessness gives birth to beginning gives birth to arrays of identity organisations, a flow that works both ways. From the apparently relatively stable identity formation we call ourselves, we can dip into beginning, into namelessness pre-beginning and, to some extent, become creative partners in re-formation, further individuation along distinction–union continuums.

Kabbalah frequently associates creation with *Chochma*, wisdom, and the God-names, YAH and YHVH. *Chochma* the father, *Binah* the mother—wisdom and understanding. One vision story sees in *Chochma* a primordial point, a kind of Big Bang, everything growing out of a primordial blast from that point. The *Zohar* describes this point as impenetrable darkness that shines with blinding radiance. On one level, it is a beginning of mind, of thought. *Binah* (understanding) and *Daat* (knowledge) mine it. In a broader sense, it gives us the insight that this universe, our world, all of existence, our very beings are made with wisdom and wisdom is part of our nature. Wisdom is part of all we see. Wisdom is part of who we are and need and want to be. Wisdom runs through us, our capacities. It is a pool we drink from and seek, a source of nourishment. Without wisdom, what would life be like? However, it is possible to be wisdom-starved, famished, endlessly hungry. In this life, things can go wrong and we can dry up. Some cannot stand it and kill themselves. Life can be too much or not enough, stillborn or aborted. There is only so much one can bear. In therapy, we try to help someone in this pass find a passage through death, an opening, a sense that there is a pool that one can dip into, bathe in. But we know from the God names of our world that once creation begins, there is always possibility of failure. In the Bible, even God threatens to wipe existence out, as if it never were. A negative force we share.

We get a sense, even from a little glimpse of creation stories in the Bible and their mystical and associative elaborations, of diverse tendencies working with and against each other in myriad ways. One way Kabbalah organises this bountiful multiplicity involves a notion of balance. Male tendencies on the right side of the tree, feminine on the left, interactive equilibrium down the middle.

An example often given is *Chesed* (mercy) on the right, *Gevurah* (judgement) on the left, and *Tiferet* (beauty) in the middle (Figure 1, p. 3). Kindliness is important but without "judgement" it lacks a certain strength. Similarly, *Gevurah*, judgement, is important but without kindness it can verge on cruelty. A balance might be something like love with strength and good judgement and *vice versa*. Beauty, partly, refers to harmonious balancing of tendencies that could tear at each other *in extremis*. More than static balance, which would become lifeless, is involved. Metaphor demonstrates a similar structure, in so far as two diverse terms are brought together, making a creative third. Creative interaction between what might otherwise be competing or even antagonistic tendencies comes to the fore. The *sephirot* mark tendencies that can enter into varied relationships, at times approaching war, yet basically and potentially co-nourishing.

There are stories of prior creations that did not work because of lack of balance. In some versions, too much mercy, in others, too much judgement. Ours works more or less, it is claimed, and still exists by virtue of better balance between a multiplicity of capacities, states, tendencies. An interactive nature of life's diversity is emphasised for growth of creativeness and even for survival. In this, Kabbalah shares something with Taoism.

* * *

The third triangle of the *sephirot* I sometimes call the Freudian triangle. It all depends on interpretation. I associate *Netzach* with endurance, persistence, *Hod* with flexibility, openness, *Yesod* with fecundity. In Kabbalah, the latter is linked with the phallus. Recently, writers try to make *Yesod* less gendered, associating it with genitals, and you see my evasive term fecundity, which stays true to the creative thrust of the whole. However, it must be admitted that there is much that is gendered and parochial in the source texts. Images and statements often are extravagant, sometimes bizarre. Yet, there is much that is profoundly electrifying and transformative if one can find one's own key.

Netzach and *Hod* are associated with prophecy. One reason is they receive from the other *sephirot* above them. Each *sephira* is feminine in relation to the one above it and masculine in relation to the one below it. Giving and receiving is a basic structure. Each *sephira* receives and gives. Endurance takes on a deeply spiritual meaning in terms of depth of receiving. The cries of the psalms, "How Long, how long, O Lord!", cries from the heart, aching for the Divine Presence. Patience and persistence are important on a survival level as well as spiritual. Levinas (1999; Eigen, 2005) brings out the importance of waiting on the unknown for creativity in human relationships. Bion writes of the importance of an analyst staying in what Klein called a paranoid–schizoid position, tolerating fragmentation, splitting, sitting with bits and pieces until a pattern spontaneously forms. A pattern again destined to fall apart, starting from scratch.

Hod I link with flexibility, openness to new experience. On a spiritual level, new relationships with God, often ecstatic. Together with *Nezach's* endurance and persistence and patience, *Hod's* flexibility adds an important ingredient on the level of practical survival as well as spiritual development. The interaction of *Hod* and *Netzach* can be fecund, fertile (*Yesod*), giving birth to further divine and earthly potential. This triangle connects with Freudian drives and the persistence and elasticity that goes with realisation. A fecundity that is a thread through many levels of experience.

I noted above that Bion's depiction of Klein's paranoid–schizoid position goes with *Netzach*. His depiction of her depressive position goes with *Hod*. Disorganised bits and pieces congeal into a whole, momentary or enduring. A gestalt, a complex organisation of parts. In psychoanalysis, this can be a moment of *Chochma* in *Hod*—aha, now I see something. Now I see a lie I lived. Now I see a greater truth. In *Hod* this can be a self-transcending vision, a moment of inspiration where things come together. Wow! I didn't see this before. On a psycho-spiritual plane, it could be a burst of glory: "Holy, holy, holy is the Lord of hosts. The whole earth is filled with His glory". If *Tiferet* is openness to beauty, *Hod* is openness to glory (think, too, of the adjective "glorious").

In psychoanalysis, *Hod* can bring freeing vision with depressive elements. Just as I experience how good life can be, I see even more clearly how bad it is. A taste of glory uplifts daily realities; at the same time, it brings glory down to earth, tasting and facing everyday reality. With the added boost and courage of *Hod*, for the first time (again) I see I am worse off than I thought I was. I see everything that is wrong with me more fully. It is harder to escape by pretending I am not the person I am. In *Hod* psychoanalysis, the sheer magnitude of destruction and wounds floor one, but, at the same time, builds more capacity to tolerate this important and often transformative moment. It can be a crucial part of growth to be brought to the point of recognising all the brokenness in oneself and existence that calls for repair, whether repair is possible or not. A moment that happens again and again. A bringing together of *Netzach* and *Hod* in *Yesod* might develop into fecund vision and attempts at creative repair. An impossible task to complete, perhaps, but a necessary one to begin.

*   *   *

One may view the *sephirot* as a structure made up of structures, processes made up of processes. Structures within structures, processes within processes. Interlacing distinction–union patterns.

They can be taken as descriptions of God's inner processes, God's divine capacities and emanations, an inherent part of God (if God has parts), a kind of body of God (if God has body). Also, they can be taken as tools God uses to create the world. They can be posited to work as filter systems .

Chassidic thought sees the *sephirot*, too, as human capacities, ways we work. In an inner way, we meld *ayin* (nothingness) and *yesh* (being), now more fully one or the other. We nullify ourselves, empty out through *ayin*, come back renewed through *yesh*. To a certain extent, we parallel and share aspects of the way God works. We are part of the way God works. To be made in God's image means we mirror or reflect or channel processes we have in common. God may be unknowable but we share ways He manifests through us.

For example, *Chochma* can be viewed as a divine or human capacity, a way of working we share, surely with differences. Divine *Chochma* involves Wisdom fully that human wisdom tastes. One wonders, does God share our appetite for wisdom, have unique appetite of His own, or is He always fully satisfied? We can never get enough wisdom and perhaps it is exciting to think that God, too, in his Infinite Creativity, also craves more. Perhaps not quite the same quality of craving as we have on earth.

We think of heaven as a place beyond more and less, a place where there can be no further good, unless Goodness, too, has a quality of creating ever more inconceivable goodness. Perhaps in heaven, too, there is no end to the Inconceivable.

We can view *Chochma* as divine revelation or pure intuition. We can look at it as pure reason or intellect, with Aristotle or Kant. By the time revelation reaches *Netzach*, it takes the form of prophecy. On another level, it can be part of practical intellect, associated with drives, ambition, goals, purpose, determination, stick-to-it-ness. There is strength in endurance, patience, know-how, learning. A *Gevurah* element runs through all the capacities. Strength is needed to be kind or loving, or striving or understanding. Strength is needed to think deeply, to procreate in a full way, to speak and act in a full way. Each of the capacities informs and qualifies the others.

Overall, the capacities are grouped according to a broad tripartite scheme, broadly following the perceived or imaged body. Roughly, head, middle, bottom; intellect, emotion, action. One can see parallels with Jung's intuition, thinking, feeling, sensation. Or Husserl's transcendental, psychological, and empirical egos. There are, too, rough parallels with Kundalini *chakras*. It is an ancient division, seen in Plato and Aristotle, who, in their own ways, depict a ladder of movement from sensation through intellect–intuition. Relevant, too, is Plato's vision of everything in the universe imaged in all souls, that we are all microcosms of everything else and need to become more fully aware of our capacities. There is an orphic tinge to Kabbalah too. In the ancient mysteries, one moves from being entombed by the body to higher eternal realms, from darkness to light. In some mysteries there are rituals in which the supplicant is put in a frightening position, a dark cave like a tomb, left alone with spectres. In the morning, the tomb is opened to the rising sun and one feels a rise of transcendent spirit. Freud remarked in a letter to Fliess that psychonalysis is akin to the ancient mysteries, allowing more freedom from instinctual domination, from lower to highter ("Where id is, there ego will be"). The rebirth theme is easily recognised in Jesus' death–resurrection, a basic rhythm the soul goes through moment to moment and over a lifetime (Eigen, 2004, 2011).

Taken in all, the *sephirot* express a rich array of human capacities, states, tendencies, Wisdom, intellect, intuition, understanding, knowing, loving, judging, sense of beauty, splendour, patience, endurance, flexibility, majesty, inspiration, openness, pro-creative, action in many forms—and all the variations, combinations, additional meanings that have accrued over the years. A tree bristling with life. Meditating on it as a whole or any of its parts can light you up, bring you to places you may need to go, open visions of the human spirit. One can also meditate on what is beyond the tree, beyond possible comprehension, dimensions wordlessly touching infinities of soul.

I have mostly written about the *sephirot* in a positive way, a positive Tree of Life or Faith or Knowing. But these capacities, too, can work in negative ways, wreak havoc, sow evil, lead to self-destruction: a negative tree. Kabbalah calls this capacity "the other side". A term with complex meaning, since it is also used to describe spiritual progress, as when Abraham passes to the other side of the river, from idol worship to the One. In Buddhism, the passage to the other side, samsara to nirvana. But in the context of the dark side, the evil side, Kabbalah sets a task: to vanquish, transform, repair. A challenge is to learn how to use our god-given capacities well, to become partners with our capacities.

One can depict a positive tree and minus tree. This is very like Bion speaking of love (L), hate (H), and knowledge (K) in both positive and negative aspects. He posits $-L$, $-H$, $-K$ as capacities working in reverse, undoing personality rather than adding or building, destroying rather than creating. A good deal of Bion's work examines processes that seek to undo themselves, obstruct positive change, destroy mind and feeling and being (Eigen, 2011). Bion's grid depicting the growth of capacity, growth, and use of thought, intuition, or feeling can work in reverse, undoing thought, intuition, feeling. Minus capacities, a minus grid. Bion notes that a good deal of use of capacities goes into discovery and repair. He goes into some detail of ways a psychoanalyst needs to keep intuition in good repair. Dramas of dual tendencies, deep faith meeting destructive force.

I mentioned earlier that Kabbalists posit prior worlds before ours that destroyed themselves because of lack of balance. It is hoped we will avoid self-destruction by better interaction of capacities. For this, it might be necessary to learn how to work with "the other side", the negative tree or grid, in ways that benefit the whole, as well as partnership between positive functions. We ought not take use or function for granted. We need to keep developing psycho-spiritual taste buds to get a helpful sense of how we are using ourselves.

Kohut (1971) speaks of "deterioration products". A psyche that fails to find support in development can, in important ways, begin to deteriorate. Aspects of self-feeling and psychic functioning can begin to go under and suffer chronic partial deaths or deformations. He uses a term, "self-object", to denote a function of support for self-building, be it another person, interest, object, or oneself. Sometimes, I picture all the capacities of the *sephirot* as a fan, they fan out revealing themselves, and we have to be good enough self-objects for our *sephirot* to keep them in good repair. What Bion says about a need to keep intuition in good repair might apply to all our capacities in their use and function. We need to do a lot of sensing–feeling–thinking to learn how to keep our *sephirot* in good repair.

* * *

The tenth and lowest *sephira*, *Malchut*, is associated with the Tree of Knowledge of Good and Evil. Mitchel Becker speaks of "the human treasure and fright of 'choice'—which can only exist in the meeting of good and bad" (posted on my online Yahoo workshop, May 2013). *Malchut*, "Kingdom", is our earth time–space realm, what we usually call the real world. Matt (2004) in his diagram of the *sephirot*, calls this domain, *Shechinah*, God's feminine presence, daughter of *Binah*. A sculpture by Anselm Kiefer depicts the *Shechinah* in a torn, tattered, scorched bridal dress. The *Shechinah*, like the Holy Spirit, is with us in our torn lives, with us in our pain and joys. There are texts in which *Binah* mothers everything into being and *Shechinah* is with us in spirit. *Yaweh*, through and as *Chochma*, seeds *Binah*, the great mother of the *sephirot*. Birth and beginnings do not end there. *Shechinah* as shepherd is a kind of guardian and witness of being, fostering more being. A Holy Presence lifting us in spirit, a comforter, restoring our soul, life seeking and finding more life as new levels of being come into view.

Why kingdom? One of my responses involves words from the Lord's prayer: Our Father in heaven, thy kingdom come, thy will be done, on earth as it is in heaven. To translate this into Kabbalah vision, prayer helps bring the soul to heaven and heaven to earth. Godly heaven in the earthly soul.

One might also say earthly soul in Godly heaven. Kabbalah–Chassidus delineates five souls, to some degree following Aristotle and Plato. In *Malchut*, the lowest level, our level, is the vital, animal soul attached to materiality. Through prayer and good deeds it can ascend to higher levels of soul, a journey of transformation.

Whatever is rigid about the Kabbalah, it is also very fluid. Multiplicities of meanings and possibilities flourish. Beginnings is a basic structural process that runs through it. Whatever awful thing happens, something more happens, something further can begin. Birth and creativity on many levels is an essential part of the weave. Birth and creativity never stop. They continue through the most awful deaths and monstrosities.

Shechinah, for example, condenses blends of possibilities. Bride of God in her resplendent attire, never ending radiance, manifest as inconceivable beauty, Sabbath bride, in her burnt, ripped by grief gown. Holy Presence with us in our brokenness, in the brokenness of creation. I think of Leonard Cohen's line, there is a crack in everything, that's how the light gets in. Perhaps, like Jesus or Akiva, *Shechinah* is always being crucified and torn by what we do to each other, what we do to ourselves.

Shechinah, too, is known as bride of Jacob, associated with *Tiferet* (beauty), and consort of Joseph, associated with *Yesod* (foundation, phallus, fecundity)—the two middle *sephirot* above her. The more you study Kabbalah, the more meanings mount. *Yesod*, God's penis, phallic power, pointing up or down, spiritual aspiration, elevation, yet impregnating existence with possibility and concern. Its creative powers uniting with *Shechinah* to replenish the earth and the human spirit. Kabbalah has a lot of sexual imagery. As mentioned earlier, I often look at *Netzach–Hod–Yesod* as the Freudian triangle, meldings of Eros and Spirit. Eros can lift the animal soul to a higher plane, in preparation for still further ascent.

Malchut is associated with David, who, in his psalms, calls out to God from the depths, over and over. One theme of the psalms is utter dependence on God, "from You is all". David links with *Shechinah* in her capacity as witness, presence, heart-broken care and capacity for endless renewal. Chassidus says that *Malchut/Shechinah* has nothing of her own but receives from the *sephirot* above it. A meaning is that in *Malchut* we come to acknowledge depths of ultimate dependence which is part of renewal. In our emptiness and nullification, we are being filled by everything, impregnated, transformed. Recently, a woman I work with said, "God is always changing us."

*   *   *

Winnicott (1988) (Eigen, 2009) writes of the importance of absolute dependence of the infant on a mother it might not know is there. Not only for physical survival, but survival of many psychical qualities. Winnicott feels that a capacity to be alone depends on the mother's supporting certain alone moments of the infant. The infant builds a sense of background support for its states. I call this background support the infant is unaware of a sense of unknown, boundless support. If enough support is not there, aloneness could be wounded. Wounded aloneness can have many repercussions, among them addictive tendencies as ways of seeking the missing support (Eigen, 2011).

Kabbalah points out the importance of needing to balance diverse tendencies, so that they can work together in well enough ways, with varying degrees of harmony. Nothing is perfect. But extremes of disharmony for long enough periods can tear the fabric of personality and society apart. Too much dependence, particularly wrong kinds of dependence, can infantilise, even cripple, a person. In some situations, a baby might need to seek what nourishment it can in emotionally toxic and damaging conditions (Eigen, 1999, 2001). A balance of dependent and independent tendencies is important or, better, creative development and interaction of these tendencies.

As mentioned earlier, Kabbalah speaks of prior worlds that failed because of imbalance of tendencies. Too much and too little of one or another capacity in extreme led to lack of interactive care and ability, resulting in deterioration and, finally, self-destruction. There are many states and capacities that come to the fore in one or another moment that need their due in order to prosper. The background support aloneness needs is one such moment. In another moment, another mood, the baby might be active, seeking contact, alive and kicking. The reality of one state does not make another state less real. William Blake felt all states are eternal. That may be an extreme way of saying many states count. Blake also describes heaven as a place where all voices express themselves maximally with results creative for all. Well, that may be a rare occurrence on earth, but the principle is worth meditating on.

Aspects of Kabbalah and psychoanalysis agree on the importance of creative interaction between apparently competing states, love and hate, for example. Bion notes that each state contributes another window on the world, another way of seeing. Sometimes I imagine our emotional lives as something like a living being with thousands of legs or arms, pulling in many directions, each with something important to contribute, something that might be needed in one or another situation. A little like having thousands of souls. How can we give all of them their due? What kind of overarching attitude are we called upon to develop, so that a frame of reference open and large enough could develop. The Passover Seder speaks of four different children, representing four personalities and ways of experiencing, one wise, one rebellious, one shy, one simple. Yet, all have a place at the Seder. They are part of the mystical community. But what if there are not just four, but infinities of soul nuances, infinities of Elijahs knocking on our door seeking care? How do we embrace and enable all we have to offer?

Yes, of course we have to be realistic. There is always lack and something unfulfilled. Everything is subject to processes of selection; everything is partial. There is always mourning for loss, what is not and cannot be. Yet, it makes a difference to what extent we have a wish to include, support, help, although we meet our limits daily.

* * *

Another factor that Kabbalah and psychoanalysis join in emphasising involves our relation to our own emotional intensity or energy, pressures of our own being. Not just a matter of imbalance (although that plays a role), but one related to how much life can we bear, how much of ourselves can we take.

Let us look again at the image of God trying to create tools (e.g., *sephirot*) through which to create the world and the tools breaking as he tries to create them, breaking from creative pressures. This scenario suggests we are endangered by our own creative energies, like a bull in a china shop. We use words that informally suggest this, for example, "stroke". A stroke of good luck, a new idea—or breaking a blood vessel, having a heart attack because of a sudden jolt. Emotional heart attacks and strokes we deal with throughout a lifetime.

In many ways, we suffer damage and damage ourselves in order to live. Injuring ourselves is part of living. What Freud calls the life

drive damages life itself in order to live. The Kabbalah vessels breaking under the impact of creation they are meant to mediate provides
a good image for what it feels like to be alive in one of its aspects. It
is a theme that comes alive in psychoanalysis, which tunes into the
difficulties we face in bearing our psyche. My psyche is too much for
me; I am too much for me.

In one passage, Bion (1994a, pp. 167–169) writes about a woman he
feels cannot bear the "urge to exist":

> I think this is again part of the fundamental story that she can't toler-
> ate being all alone with her self even when she is with other people.
> This 'self' won't leave her—it goes with her. But we don't know what
> this 'self' is—it certainly isn't a self that she wants to be alone with, so
> she is always reaching out for somebody else. If she couldn't come to
> you she would certainly go to someone else: if she couldn't find
> anyone else, she would find a crowd of people in London, anywhere
> where there are masses of people so as to avoid being aware that she
> is with her self whether she likes it or not.
>
> It is difficult to describe what she is talking about, but I feel it is a sort
> of 'urge to exist'. And this urge is completely indifferent to human
> beings; it doesn't care whether we die in childbirth or in any other
> way. Her parents' urge to exist forced them to give birth to a child
> whether they wanted one or not. So she herself is a product of that
> same urge and is at its mercy. She is frightened of being all alone with
> that urge to exist which doesn't mind what happens to her—it is
> completely ruthless. And she is terrified of being a slave to the urge as
> her parents were. In a similar way bacilli and viruses are completely
> indifferent to human beings. If we are wiped out, another kind of
> 'thing' will exist instead.

An earlier remark Bion made in this section: "We seem to be the kind
of animal that has to have a society; we depend on it and are all alone
at the same time. It is true at the age of forty, at the age of four, and
at the age of nought" (p. 167).

For some, being alone is more difficult than being with others, for
some the reverse. For some, both. How to live with and appreciate our
double capacities is a perennial challenge. For some, to bear a self, to
bear society, is more than they can bear.

Part of therapeutic emphasis involves building capacity to bear a
psyche, to suffer experience and even, Bion suggests, to suffer joy.

This, in part, is a profound elaboration of Freud's often dismissed depictions of difficulties in bearing stimulation, especially emotional impacts.

Not being able to bear a baby is part of this. This theme is elaborated by Winnicott (1992; Eigen, 1993, 2009, 2012b, 2013) as well as Bion. How much of the baby can a mother take without getting damaged or retaliating or sinking and collapsing? How much of myself can I take without deforming, breaking, hiding, or going to bed? Not being able to bear a baby has added components like wear and tear, fatigue, changing demands, responsibility dread and guilt, anger at impingement, sense of inadequacy, threats to safety and being, threats to our selves. Emotional components are part of it with all the difficulties involved in supporting emotional life, its ambushes and needs.

I have worked with parents who were afraid of killing their children. Not being able to bear can turn into an urge to kill to tone down the unbearable. How much killing is an attempt to escape the unbearable?

Psychoanalysis challenges us to build capacity to support emotional life without resorting to violence—although experiencing emotional life itself can be violent. Some go through more than they can bear in order to grow. I suspect the possibility of growth in the face of, and while undergoing, destructive impacts is part of what led Bion to posit Faith as the psychoanalytic attitude. There are ways, I fear, that faith can grow by being ripped apart. Faith that strengthens by being nulled, that takes us to unanticipated places when there is no cause for it to exist at all.

How do we prosper as a human life form and not extinguish ourselves through misuse of capacities or insufficient ability to work with our capacities? It might not even be maliciousness that does us in, but incapacity to work with our capacities. How do we learn to use our amazing capacities to enrich planet Earth and ourselves? Both Moses and Freud ask, "Can we do it?" Psychoanalysis targets an emotional component and ways to work with it, ways very much open to personal and intersubjective experiment. In *Feeling Matters* (2007), I wrote, "As long as feelings are second class citizens, people will be second class citizens". What we *can* do with ourselves is, at this moment, in question. The sheer immensity of our gifts sometimes paralyses us. Undreamt of capacities keep emerging. They keep growing. New does not stop. Are we up to the task? I think it a relief to say,

I don't know, or even no, and stop pretending. A big theme in Kabbalah and therapy is repair—but do we know what to repair or how? There are a lot of ways to be broken. It is a frightening but freeing vision that capacities break as we use them and sometimes, through breaking, develop more. There is something in us that keeps chipping away at the limits of the possible, while haunted by a state of psychic indigestion.

* * *

The main character in the *Zohar* is Rabbi Shimon bar Yohai, a *tzadik* who lived in the first century. Some religious groups to this day consider him its author and celebrate the day of his death (*Lag B'Omer*). Some say the *Zohar* began when Rabbi Yohai and his son Eliezar hid in a cave for twelve years, escaping Roman persecution. He was a disciple of Rabbi Akiva, who was executed by the Romans (Eigen, 2012a). The second temple had been destroyed and Jews who taught and practised were at risk. Modern historians attribute authorship of the *Zohar* to Moshe de Leon, who lived in thirteenth-century Spain, although it is likely that some other authors of that time also contributed. There are stirring stories of Moshe de Leon channelling Rabbi Shimon's spirit in a process of profound soul transmission. He seemed to write tracts a little at a time and tried to sell them as they were written, so the *Zohar* is loosely organised with no official version.

The *Zohar* is an imaginative elaboration of stories, dialogues and events growing from meditation on aspects of Torah. Some thought it a hidden Torah, a bringing out of deeper truths. While aspects of Kabbalah can be bizarre, parochial, off-putting, many passages hit you from behind, igniting sudden illumination that grows and draws you in to close study. Roustang (1980) wrote a book entitled, *Psychoanalysis Never Lets Go*. For those susceptible, or in need, or so disposed, the *Zohar* never lets go either. It grows and grows.

I do not think it is simply a meditation on Torah. The author throws everything into it but the kitchen sink. It is a wonderful amalgam of varied traditions. One can see Plato, Aristotle, Orpheus, and ancient mysteries, Muslim and Christian mystics, Jewish scholars and mystics, and much more. My advice is find passages or even phrases or words that speak to you and stick with those. The more you look, the more you feel and see. There is a spiritual hunger in this work that can make you hungry, lead you to green pastures, free your mind.

Whether you are an orthodox observer or a spiritual free-loader, there is something for you. Sometimes you will be baffled, and sometimes you will feel that you came upon a warm hearth after a long journey.

The *Zohar* can have paradoxical effects. If you practise religion "literally", it can make you even more observant in a deeper, fuller way. It can bring out deeper meaning of the laws, deepen already deep faith, or return you to faith in deeper ways, open you with hidden meaning. On the other hand, it helped someone like me be less observant, freer from "literal" religion, more able to explore and value creative possibilities for myself.

I once came upon a tract in which Rabbi Schneerson, leader of the Lubavitch Chassidim, explained that God could make the world look as if it was millions or billions of years old, while actually existing for about 5000–6000 years. He offered this as a possible reason why scientists were fooled—because God fooled them. It was a moment when Rabbi Schneerson's hold on me went "puff". Just like that, I began to feel freer to think my own thoughts, feel my own feelings, my own visions.

I still read his insights avidly. They speak to my depths. He was one of the few people in my life with whom I had an experience of seeing myself when I looked at him. He has absorbed and transmuted Torah and Jewish mysticism and much else. Much of what he said and wrote deepened my sense of spirit. And yet—"puff"—in an instant the shell of "literal" observance began to dissolve and I felt an inner vise begin to loosen.

Life is complex and many factors went into contributing a sense that faith is something deeper than any specific set of rituals or codes. Bion (1970) speaks of a big bang of the psychological universe and Matt (1998) a big bang of the spiritual universe. They overlap, intersect, expanding the possible.

Now, more and more authors say there is less contradiction between religion and science, if you view them certain ways. Bion (1970, 1990, 1994b) often writes of quantum theory and faith, although aspects of the faith he points to might be deeper than what is usually called religion. What can that mean, faith deeper than religion?

* * *

A theme that recurs in this book and the one before it (Eigen, 2012a) is brokenness and repair. Some even say God is broken. In psychoanalysis, Tustin writes of a broken heart in infancy (Eigen, 2012a). A broken heart at the core of existence. As we said, tools God used to create existence partly shattered under His impact. We are told our job is to repair the broken *sephirot*, the broken tools, a broken God. And we can do that by repairing ourselves.

Yet, for this we need help, God's help, our help. And what is there to guarantee that it can be done? What guarantees that God will not once more shatter under His own impact, that we will not shatter? Is this like Sisyphus, endless shatter and repair? I do not know about ultimates, what finally happens or will happen to anyone or anything. I do not know the end to any story. But I do know that acts of repair can open new paths of experience. Whatever relative success or not, acts of repairing can take you to places you never touched before. In some sense, the Wound that Never Heals motivates spontaneous movement towards and discovery of precious moments of experience. The never-ending wound spurs never-ending development. Making us more than we could have been otherwise. Somewhere, there is a turn, a shift, from partners in repair to partners in creation. Wounded partners in creation, perhaps, but something more, something else. Eternal light shining through the eternal wound is one moment. Healing as an opening of new dimensions is another. Opening to the new can itself be healing or an important part of it.

A wounded, healing partnership is something different from public, political models. A public posture is to act more whole than one really feels, to pretend to be stronger, know more, be more confident than reality can bear. A semi-universal social pretence to be better than one is. It is important to have places to crumble, bend over in pain, and cry from one's heartbreak, one's yearnings. Perhaps therapy and religious prayer, at least sometimes, touch this place.

* * *

The erotic is one dimension of repair. Like so many capacities, it can work in reparative, creative, and destructive modes. The sexual act is a reparative act, or can be. It can heal, make one feel more whole. In contrast with the idea or fear of the penis being damaging, Klein pictures it as repairing a sense of damage in the woman, making her feel more whole. Sexual acts, especially when I was younger, made me feel more worthy.

There is much in the *Zohar* about not being whole without male–female interlocking, a shared mystical bone that connects the sexes. This sounds a little like Bion noting the linking function of penis and breasts. The *Zohar* and aspects of Jung are an easy fit. Both take connection to further dimensions, emphasising internal union, an internal wedding of male–female aspects of personality.

In the *Zohar*, the image of sexual intercourse reaches many levels. One of *Shechinah's* mates is *Yesod*, *Yahweh's* phallus. Erotic communion between *Yesod* and *Shechinah* helps to repair *Shechinah*. Erotic and spiritual repair are one.

Yesod is associated with Joseph, called a dreamer and righteous. He helped, but did not sleep with, Egypt. He is viewed as part of a "pillar of righteousness" that runs through the Kabbalah tree. Phallic like the spine, upright. Joseph is seen as narcissistic by many, but life takes him deeper than narcissism. The coat of many colours includes the palette of feelings in life and a positive attitude to people. It is God's rainbow covenant set above. He is a dreamer and has a talent for interpreting dreams, with God's help. Like his many-coloured coat, he straddles worlds. He comes through many negative aspects of experience, in the end, standing on his feet. He is *Shechinah's* husband. Part of their procreative activity is to bring souls closer to God, as David says, "my heart cries out for the living God". Life at one of its most profound moments. Through Joseph and *Shechinah*, one draws closer to God, inner union, inner fruitfulness.

A triple movement of unification occurs (more, but we'll stick with triple). (1) Joseph unites with *Shechinah* (*Malchut*), a union *between sephirot* (one could also use Bion's term, linking, creation of links). The emphasis here is on making, building, formation, akin to Freud's Eros. (2) This helps stimulate linking *within Shechinah* (*Malchut*). David is associated with *Malchut*, and pro-creates with *Shechinah*, union within *Malchut*. The singer, poet, and warrior who brings us close to God. His songs are worlds of emotions that traverse how far and near to God we can feel. Perhaps, he takes us as close as we can get. Except that life takes us closer. David, if anything, is a man of life, this life, the vicissitudes of *Malchut*, the kind of closeness to God that can only happen through *Malchut*. No other quality is like it. (3) Some say Jacob (*Tiferet*) is the true husband of *Shechinah* (*Malchut*) and Joseph (*Yesod*) helps mediate this union as well. Joseph, or the spirit, sense, feeling meant here, is the vehicle for a triple unification, a tri-wedding, inner union: Jacob, Joseph, and David, all pro-creative mates with *Shechinah*. The *sephirot* are all about creating, forming, life's generative impulse on countless planes. Procreation as a symbol applies to real movements of the soul and spirit. *Yesod* as Foundation emphasises diverse possibilities of generative distinction–union. You can meditate on couplings of the *sephira* in all sorts of ways, limited only by your capacity for speculative imagination. Imaginings unlock realities. If you discover capacities not covered by the *sephirot*, explore them, experience where they take you. Make your own tree, your own grid categories.

Sexual linking as a sign of renewal, making new babies of mind and spirit. Meltzer (2008) often refers to psychoanalytic babies, expressive of psychological birth processes and dramas of union and difference. Sexual experience can take you to new places, as can dimensions of life symbolised by sexual generation. The concept of inner union of capacities, souls, and worlds draws heavily on erotic images, even if they go beyond them.

As suggested above, there are unknown dimensions of repair and discovery awaiting fecund moments. New dimensions opened by exercising our psycho–erotic–spiritual equipment. Perhaps we cannot expect full repair of the eternal wound except in the world to come. But psychologically, the world to come can be the next moment, moments to come. In our work, notions of "full repair" might inhibit repair that is possible and experiences beyond the idea of repair, experiences that add to existence just by happening. The beauty of life expressed through *Tiferet* touches and uplifts us in a spontaneously intrinsic way. We do not have to add anything more to it in order to appreciate a grace received.

While repair is a profoundly human theme, emergence of new reality can leave repair behind. As mentioned before, Eros has reparative aspects and also stimulates new realities. We are often told in Chassidus that if we are not growing, opening to new realities, we are not just stagnant, but deteriorating. Not to grow is to deteriorate. Chassidus means this spiritually, growing as spiritual beings. One can also mean this psychologically. There are unifying words that span dimensions, and growth and birth are two of them.

If we put repair and emergence together, we have moments in which coming through something (difficulty, trauma, loss, defeat) can couple with an unexpected learning or opening, or taste of a world to come here and now, even, at times, tragic growth and learning.

*   *   *

Let me share a moment in which something new happened in face of death, unplanned, unpremeditated. In the background was a sense of being helped by Rabbi Schneerson's (1978) writing on the *yechida* soul. It is not something I was consciously thinking about at the time. About two years earlier, an inner prompting led me to re-read passages from his book, *On the Essence of Chassidus*, and I felt changed by the reading. I read the same book twenty-five years earlier without much happening, and now there was a decisive moment.

There are five souls in Jewish mysticism, actually more, infinities of souls. But the tracts I am thinking of list: (1) *nefesh*, a vital soul in the plane of *Malchut*, the soul of David, concerned with the eternal One here and now, planet earth, life as we know and live it: (2) *ruach*, often translated as spirit-wind, connotes our emotional soul, roughly higher and lower emotions, *sephirot* 4–9 (genitals, gut, torso, heart) (3) *neshama*, "breath", related to intellect and intuition often linked with brain, but also informally linked with heart; (4) *chaya*, "life", strad-dling *Keter* and supernal realms, intuition closer to *Ein Sof*; (5) *yechida*, "one", a dimension of soul in which our essence is in contact with God's essence. One can view these five as souls or soul dimensions, capacities, states.

I think I have always had some sense of *yechida*, but in the past two years this sense has grown in freeing ways. There were moments it lifted me above my knots, parts of personality I had all but given up on. Blocks that I banged my inner head on for years seemed to dissolve. That does not mean there is not more to go and always will be. But some essential difference happened. Reading Rabbi Schneer-son's words about the soul's essence connected with God's essence lit me from within in ways that felt curative. Some of the things I went to psychoanalysis for fifty-five years earlier lifted in a moment, although I doubt such a moment could have happened without intense and extended psychoanalytic preparation and time off from it as well. Not that I am a whole new person, cured but not cured, still wicked, wild me. But something . . .

My essence connected with God's essence. This sense has its own deepening, enriching trajectories, unpredictable, surprising, sometimes comforting, challenging. Perhaps close to what Bion means by at-onement, homelessness as deep home.

In the months before this seminar, I was helping someone die. A person scared to death of dying, not because of death, but terrified she would remain forever in her last state, which she was sure would be tormented. She was attuned to spirit, but on a psychological level severely tormented, the latter for her a spur to spiritual development. She was a Kabbalah scholar, teacher, social worker, psychotherapist, and mystic. A teaching she dreaded was that your last state would be your state for all eternity. A teaching I felt was cruel and, thus, rejected it. I do not think we should be judged or judge ourselves by a part of the whole.

Such a state could point to unrepented areas that need work. But to take the final measure of oneself by what is left undone sounds over-severe, unless it turns out to be an opening to more in the unknown to come.

For years my patient, Sara, flickered on and off between a range of tormented states and uplifting, life-affirming ones. She had been ill a long time and expected to die over fifteen years ago. She had lupus most of her adult life and further complications as she aged. Her mother died of a congenital disease in the latter's forties. Sara lived to be seventy. You can get a glimpse into some of her states in the chapter, "Alone with God" in *The Sensitive Self* (2004), where I quote her at length. She went in and out of hospital for physical treatments, often painful, for many years.

It would be hard to describe the immense intensity of her tortured moments, psychic torture that physical torture added to. And the beauty of her spiritual insights. Realities flickering back and forth. Impossible to let you know the dread of dying caught in a tormented flicker, punished forever. We did many things in the weeks before her death and then one day by phone while she was in her hospital bed, I said over and over, you can go higher than the torment. You can lift yourself higher than the torment. Go to *yechida*, straight to *yechida*. She knew what I meant but it never occurred to her to do it, or that she could do it. Or perhaps she could not find it or feared she could not find it. But in an instant, she got it. Some more flickers, and then she found the place above. Like climbing above turbulence in a plane to clear sailing. She felt at peace. We spoke that day for the last time. She died the morning of our next appointment, three days later.

At her funeral and afterwards, those close to her told me she died peacefully.

When I think of this lifting, I think of *The Gospel at Colonus* at the Brooklyn Academy of Music many years before, a black Oedipus with gospel singers. In one scene, Jesus–Oedipus, like my patient, was rising from the dead and the gospel singers sang the words, "Higher, higher, higher", as Oedipus rose, as the human spirit rose from the grave, from the grave of one's tortured body, one's tortured personality.

If I had not experienced my *yechida* moment, I doubt I could have helped Sara experience hers. I would have stayed stuck in mind–heart–gut pain, *sephirot* pain. *Yechida* took me somewhere else. You don't always have to stay with or in the turbulence. You don't always have to go through it. There are moments to rise above it, higher than the turbulence. Moments when going above the turbulence can be curative, beyond *sephirot*. Yes, constant struggle is important. One must go through what one must go through. But there is also grace, faith below, within, and above the turbulence, above the struggle, beyond the torment.

*   *   *

Who is the hero of the *Zohar*? *Ein Sof*? *Shechinah*? The human spirit? An ostensible human candidate is Rabbi Shimon, whom many Chassidim thought and still think to be the author. Moses de Leon, of twelfth-century Spain, whom scholars think to be the main author, used many Talmudic rabbis as characters in his tracts, Rabbi Shimon a central one, the main human hero, a profound spiritual hero. The book is an adventure of spirit, vicissitudes of spirit, one of the great spiritual travelogues of the amazing wisdom literature human beings have produced. Moses de Leon's imagining of Rabbi Shimon and others spans psychological, spiritual, mythopoetic levels. I sometimes call the Kabbalah one of the greatest light shows that exist, creating and exploring realms of the fabulous, opening magical, mystical realities, creating wondrous moments out of pain and joy.

Near the end of the *Zohar* is Rabbi Shimon's death. The build-up begins with the book called "the greater assembly". All of Rabbi Shimon's companions, great rabbis all, give discourses on divine secrets. They speak their mind–hearts out. Revelation as a door of repair. Here is another structure with psychoanalytic kinship, the importance of discovery and disclosure of secrets, of the hidden. It is as if the circle around Rabbi Shimon has a presentiment and time is of the essence. Revelation of secrets increases in pace. Revelation and repair. A cousin of psychoanalytic valuation of insight (*Chochma, Binah, Daat*). A sense of the secret as a structure seems part of who we are. Winnicott touches this domain with his "incommunicado core". You have Kabbalah's unknown "high spark" and Winnicott's invisible "vital spark".

Discourse in the great assembly was so intense that three of the rabbis present perished. Remember the Rabbi Akiva story in the garden? And the Rabbi Luria story of creative vessels that could not take the power of life and shattered? In the first, four seekers entered the garden: one killed himself, one went mad, one became heretical, and Rabbi Akiva emerged aglow. In the second, vessels of creation were shattered by the intensity of the creative activity they needed to mediate.

In the great assembly, three perished, but the rest survived. In the Bible, there may be great perishing, but always a seed survives. To mediate secrets, to hold, discover–create and communicate them, to be broken in the process, to be healed in the process, to be transported in unsuspected ways.

So much depends on affective attitude as a frame of reference for aspects of experience. Remember the *Zohar* insisting that if Joseph's brothers interpreted his dream differently, reality would have been different. Affective attitude makes a real difference.

Three went in and did not come out. Rabbi Akiva went in and came out. Going in and coming out, coming through. Most in the great assembly came through. Revealed what they could see and bear and came through. They survived their truths, at least for a time. Truth can kill, truth can free.

Some time later, Rabbi Shimon and his companions gathered once more—on the day of his death. A gathering called the lesser or smaller assembly. This time, Rabbi Shimon said only he would speak. Since this was his last day, he wanted to unburden himself of all the divine secrets stored within. More than unburden. Share what is hidden in the service of repair. Perhaps more than repair. Share what is within for the sake of lifting the spirit to further heights, new possibilities for the sake of heaven. He worried that such revelations might do more harm than good, but felt impelled to risk all in his last moments.

I tell the story drawing on a number of sources and my own imaginings. Do not hold any text responsible for my variations, although I am indebted to rich resources, including Mathers, *The Kabbalah Unveiled* (1887), Zahavy, *Idra Zuta Kadisha: The Lesser Holy Assembly* (1977), Liebes, *Studies in the Zohar* (1993), Matt, *Zohar: Annotated and Explained* (2002).

Rabbi Shimon begins by announcing, "Today is my wedding day". Now, up to this point, throughout the great narratives of the *Zohar*, Rabbi Shimon has mediated holiness. "Holy, holy, holy, the whole earth is filled with His glory." Who can be closer to God than Rabbi Shimon? Yet, on his wedding–death day, he confesses, insists, there is something wrong with him, something defective. He has always felt something wrong with him. What is wrong, he feels, is that he is unmarried.

In real life, Rabbi Shimon was married and had children. A son, Rabbi Eliezar, a great mystic and scholar, participated in both assemblies. In the second, he called out what Rabbi Shimon said so all could hear. Rabbi Shimon could not be alluding to his earthly marriage. It was another source of incompletion. When he says that he does not have a bride, we leave a literal realm of Eros. On this day, his death day, he will have a bride he longed for, a profoundly spiritual wedding.

To paraphrase and amplify Rabbi Shimon's words: the last time we talked, something was still missing. Today only I will speak and hopefully God will tell me what to say (as Socrates hoped, as he was dying, the Daemon would tell him what to say).

Rabbi Shimon felt afraid to say everything yet ashamed not to. Fear of punishment for holding back, fear of punishment for saying all. But a deep urge prompted him. To tell was precursor to the wedding. There was, too, a fear that not telling would deprive souls of learning what they needed for repair and heightening. Holding back would hold others back.

So he reveals what he can and arrives at a moment when he at last is going to say the one word he kept within him all this time. The conflict heightened: God wanted me to say this one word all my life and now I am not being permitted to say it. Even at this moment of revealing all, something was held back. Being stopped at the last moment recalls Abraham about to strike Isaac with a knife and his hand is stopped. Here, a knife of revelation, the tongue, is silenced. An *akedah* of the spirit.

I was with a patient who was going through something with a guru who sleeps with followers. He felt their mating would be spiritually transforming. She balked, but was tempted. Her husband and children became less real as her guru and she became sources of ecstasy for each other. I found myself holding middle ground, a sense of stability in tumult. Part of me thought, Wow!, how great!, a transforming tantric moment. But a psychoanalytic element thought: there is always lack. I envisioned the moment dying down, passing, and the impulse of erotic revelation moving on to other momentary possibilities. None of this was said, just felt. Was my unspoken state getting in the way of their reaching a higher place together? Was my picture of it leaving destruction in its wake a personal limitation or a sense of reality?

Much happened that I must leave out. We were in some muddle. Ecstasy is terrific, but was also causing terrible pain. Could she break up her marriage? Be special for a while, then drop down to one of various followers raised with her leader to another level? She also kept thinking that this ecstasy was her own, not just his. He evoked it in a heightened way, but it was something in her, her own.

One of the happenings that broke or diminished the spell was her happening upon my book, *Kabbalah and Psychoanalysis*, and reading about loving with all your heart and soul and might and a spontaneous feeling of "I love you, I love you". Something locked in and she began saying, "I love you, I love you, I love you", over and over. All of a sudden it felt that God was saying this to her. "I love you, I love you . . ." and then it snapped into place. She felt God's love all through her, "I love you" all through her.

When she came back to herself, the ecstasy-man became man-sized and her husband and children looked good again, better than ever. She felt so relieved she had gone through the experience without acting on it sexually. She could now go back to living. Something became unjammed. To me it felt as if it happened through a mixture of luck and grace. Once it happened, it happened quickly. You can be cured in an instant but a lot goes into it. In reality, you have to be "cured" again and again. It doesn't stop.

Rabbi Shimon was reaching for an inner bride. Part of his reaching involved speaking hidden words, revealing the unknown. And, at the last moment, he was prohibited from saying the one word he was meant to speak all his life. We do not know what the one word is. But you have to realise Moses de Leon, or whoever the author might be, was making the whole thing up. Like Salmon Rushdie's fiction of Mohammed. A genre of spiritual fiction, spiritual imagination, an adventure of the fabulous. Amazing parts of a mystical journey. It lights us up. It is like a match that lights the stove. No need to worship the match or stove or even the light—let them take you where they can.

Rabbi Shimon tells all the secrets he can but one. Can you find it, your own unspeakable secret—the untellable?

At last, the narrative brings us to the moment of mating, the spiritual wedding, the fullest wedding of all. Rabbi Shimon's wedding to the *Shechinah*. A great vision before he died, a marvellous variation of the love–death theme. Light concealed and revealed. That which is hidden, unseen, unknown, that which is seen and known—one and not one, separate and not separate. He feels healed, at-one, with one secret untold. Uniting with the *Shechinah*, he was whole. Something–nothing held back, a double single state. Something held back at a moment of total fulfilment, as if both aspects of human existence, the empty and full cup, are one.

A psalm near the end of the Jewish prayer service says there is none else, no one, no thing else. Akin to a moment in the *Bhagavad Gita* where Krishna shows himself as everything. There is none else. The *Zohar* has double–single logic: separate but not separate, the ancient mystery of the many and the one. We see organised processes yet experience something to which no organisation applies. Chuang Tzu speaks of identity without form. The psalmist: "God opens His hand and satisfies the desire of every living being". What is this desire, a desire always being satisfied by an open hand? And the closed hand, the concealment? Does one ever get to the bottom of what is and is not hidden? Open and closed, always–never satisfied. What an array of capacities to live with, to discover, replenish, enrich.

All divine lights imaginable, seen and unseen, shining at Rabbi Shimon's wedding. All the *sephirot* shining and all that will never be seen, invited guests. The word that cannot be uttered becomes a source for endless streaming of creativeness.

*   *   *

We speak of a ladder and rungs of enlightenment. The *sephirot* represent ascending–descending rungs of enlightenment. Any and all as basis for meditation, search, assimilation. If we start at the bottom of the Tree of Life, we start with *Malchut* and climb higher and higher. We have an enlightenment journey pointing upward through *yesod*, *hod, netzach, tiferet, gevurah, chesed* (*daat*), *binah, chochma, keter*, and beyond. We do the same with the *chakras*, which Molofsky compares to Jacob's ladder (2009). We climb the rungs of the ladder of the *sephirot* and *chakras* higher and higher, inside our bodies, souls, mind, throughout our capacities.

Yet, some spiritual leaders also speak of going directly to the goal, instantaneously and all at once. Saint Paul went back and forth between struggle and the slow climb, slippage and re-dedication to moments of grace where dualities and oppositions no longer hold. Years ago, I did rapid breathing meditation suggested by Bhagwan Rajneesh, which sometimes acted as a rapid express to higher states. Rabbi Schneerson also spoke of a direct rocket to the divine, straight to the goal region. You don't stop, you don't go to jail, you go! Rabbi Schneerson said repeatedly that this is the time, the coming of the messiah, *moshiach* (messiah) now. Whatever else this means, it refers to a state, a moment of experience, a taste of the messianic age in this instant, immediately, fully. The world to come is the next moment, and the next moment is entry to the World of Grace. The next moment is this moment, now. Always now.

We meet many possibilities, now experiencing rigidity and hardships moving from level to level, now fluidity. Being centred at different places on the tree, emphasising different capacities and attitudes, can be a source of conflict. Someone more in *netzach* or *yesod* may feel tension with a *chochma* person. Misunderstanding can take place because of differing emphases of tendencies. The deeper one goes, the more one sees that all levels are in all the others, an experience that can more readily enable access across barriers. The tree, with its worlds and capacities, gives a bird's-eye view of how where we live can foster miscommunication. Through living and practice, we catch on that we speak from different places, different levels, qualities. In Rabbi Shimon's final vision, the light of each *sephira* shines with the light of all the others, concealed and unconcealed lights, a climactic symphony. Whatever differences, generatively connected.

The wedding had many interweaving dimensions shimmering together in one flame. Male–female is a dominant part of Rabbi Shimon's vision. Each *sephira* is male or female in relation to the *sephira* above or below, female to one above it, male to the one below. You might say the wedding was made up of many weddings simultaneously, between and within all *sephirot*. I say within because, I feel, it is not just a matter of above–below, although that is a basic Kabbalah structure. Infinite and infinitesimal weddings are eternally going on within each *sephira* as well, creative links throughout micro and ultra dimensions. A vision of grand fecundity throughout creation and beyond.

Rabbi Shimon's last words expressed a sense of the One-in-many. There is none else. Perhaps nothing hurt Rabbi Shimon more than feeling lack of closeness to God, something we are told Rabbi Nachman felt so many centuries later, kinship across time (Eigen, 2012a, Chapter Two). There was a sense that Rabbi Shimon could have gone on, more and more could be seen and said. Perhaps that is where we come in, part of incessant mediating of vision and reality.

Rabbi Abbas was writing down Rabbi Shimon's words and became aware of silence. The Holy Spark was gone but such a spark lights other sparks. As I look at all of you I see many holy sparks. Is this part of what happens in therapy, sparks igniting sparks? Winnicott speaks of the vicissitudes of a vital spark. A spark vital on many levels.

When I told my wife the story of Rabbi Shimon's wedding–death day, my wife told me about a funeral of a friend of hers who committed suicide in her late twenties, nearly forty years ago. At the funeral it was snowing, and the snow was coming down and my wife felt that now her friend was married. It was as if the snow was her wedding veil and now she was complete.

*   *   *

[After a fifteen-minute break]

We spoke of spiritual representations of what cannot be represented. Bion, too, often says that he can, at best, evoke an experience but not represent it. So much about emotional life is unknown, perhaps unknowable. So much about what we call emotional problems are unsolvable. Yet, we press ourselves against experience, struggle, and often something happens. We might not solve a difficulty but find ourselves in another place. By pressuring one rung of existence, we find ourselves at another.

If we realise our representations are incomplete, partial, with many loose threads, we can find much of value in them. Or, to use, Kabbalah language, there is the unrevealed but also the revealed. Much can be done with the latter, but texts like the *Zohar* teach us that more is unknown than known. And what we know hinges on particular places we occupy, vantage points, avenues of approach. We might wish to explore what we can and participate in the creativity that informs us. But the remainder is ever humbling and invites us to keep growing. How we see and react to others, as well as ourselves, is part of the permanent challenge.

As you may know from *Kabbalah and Psychoanalysis* (2012a), in a conversation I had with Bion he remarked, "I use the Kabbalah as a framework for psychoanalysis". I think in the little time we have left I would like to begin by exploring aspects of Bion's O-grams (Figures 3 and 4, p. 10; also, Bion, 1994b, pp. 323, 325; Eigen, 2012a, Appendix 4, p. 101) and make some comparisons with the Kabbalah tree.

The Kabbalah tree, as you know, has a vertical, up–down structure, modelled on the human body. Upright posture figures heavily as part of a background to spiritual discourse. Upright refers to moral qualities, righteousness, which raises dilemmas as to what being "right" is. In *Rage* (2002), I suggest that no attitude has done more harm in human history than a sense of being "right". The above–below of body structures and the upright posture, coupled with above–below of heaven and earth, form a compelling perceptual framework from which guiding concepts grow.

Although divine mystery, power, or virtue, or energy or presence permeates everything, God or *Ein Sof* ("Without Bounds") is depicted as above the tree as well as throughout and around it. The flow of Godly presence from top down is paramount. On the other hand, Bion's "tree", or O-grams, go from bottom up. O or unrepresentable, unknown ultimate reality is alone at the bottom, the unknown, perhaps unknowable, source. Readers of Bion are aware of his penchant for reversals. He, like many others, noted the God–dog symmetry. "God" strikes me as a fairly impoverished word, in spite of its nearly endless cultural associations. Its common usage often blocks access to the reality it seeks to mediate. *Ein Sof* is one try to evoke the uncommunicable, the mystery of contact with what cannot be known. Bion's O is not identical with *Ein Sof*, although the two notations have resonances.

I coined the term "O-gram" for ease of usage. It is not a term Bion used, but a liberty I have taken. As I suggested, O and *Ein Sof* are structural correlatives of their respective systems, although not identical. Like *Ein Sof*, O may be unknown but has impacts. In psychoanalysis, it is a notation for the unknown emotional reality of a session, of a life. Sometimes, Bion uses it to suggest catastrophic impact at the point of origin, O, of personality. We read the effects of O like tea leaves, we read displacements, imprints, residues, signals. For example, we piece pictures together from trauma signals. Winnicott (1992; Eigen, 2004, 2009) has a related description of trauma hitting as personality begins to form, and in sessions we dip into bits of trauma in derivative form, trying to make contact with ourselves more deeply.

Bion is cautious about pictures we put together. We often react to our pictures of people rather than an actual person before us, sometimes with bad results. We take our picture as more real than the person. That is one reason he advises trying to be without expectation, memory, understanding, or desire, always starting from scratch. No, we cannot rid ourselves of ourselves and our capacities, and I doubt that we should. Better to develop, enrich, grow, learn to be with and use ourselves better or, as Beckett says, "fail better". Still, there is a tendency that works towards cleaning ourselves out in order to give fresh intuition space. One meaning I give to Bion's O is becoming more Open.

Think about it in concrete human relations. Suppose one justifies reactive tendencies by thinking, "I know what this person is like". "I know what my wife is like". Not exactly a good attitude for promoting creative interactions. With O, the ultimate emotional reality of a situation unknown and unrepresentable, there is always room for more or something else to happen. O has this in common with *Ein Sof*, which, among its depictions, is infinite potential.

O for open. *Ein Sof*—no limit. Open is a big word in Kabbalah. Open your gates and let the divine spirit enter. Many scenes in the *Zohar* begin by saying one or another rabbi opens, meaning opens a discussion. Not just opens a discussion in the sense of starting, but opening also in the sense of opening something that is closed, open a box, a block, a path, a hand, a mind or soul or heart. The gates open, the gates close. A kind of rhythm, opening–closing. Lacan depicts a rhythm of the unconscious by speaking of pulsations from a slit.

William Blake writes of creation happening in pulsations, likening a creative moment to a pulse beat.

In the *Zohar*, once a discussion opens, many chime in opening possibilities. Something we are doing now, to this day, this moment. I never cared for the part of the Yom Kippur service when the gates begin to close. I tend to feel they are always open, always closed, part of an opening–closing rhythm, psychic pulse. Your constitution at the moment plays a role in how far a gate is open or not. We can be partially open and closed at the same time. I suspect that is more the rule than all or nothing. Open in one way, closed another, not wholly one or the other. Perhaps that is a reason why Rabbi Shimon had a whole experience on his wedding–death day—he had to die to have a whole experience. We speak of the kiss of death. Shimon dying when kissed by *Shechinah*, embraced by O, all the lights on and off at the same time.

We are partial beings, mixed, although we may have more whole-ish moments and visions. O, the unknown, manifesting in partial ways. You can fill in the blank any way that is congenial to you—if you like, we can call it Ounknown dynamic process. But whatever we call it will not exhaust it.

*   *   *

Bion's first O-gram (Image 3, p. 10; Bion, 1994b, p. 323) has O alone at the bottom giving rise to Root, which branches out to Instrument, God, Stone, Language, Paint, which, respectively, give rise to Music, Religion, Sculpture, Poetry, Painting. You might call this an expressive O-gram, diagramming as it does emergent capacities concerned with feeling. Any aspect of the network can be of great importance to a person. Bion asks, "What is important? The root? The flower? The germ? The conflict? The durability?" The list can be expanded. Depending on time and situation, capacities can nourish or conflict with each other. Conflicts can be creative and/or destructive. It is often hard, if not impossible, to discern what leads to what. Bion depicts structural processes that inform human life from early in history until now. All the categories, at one or another time, play roles in emotional expressiveness, O-expressions.

In Kabbalah, *Ein Sof* at the top; with Bion, O at the bottom. Both concerned with Origins. For Bion, sub-origins, sub-O, sub-roots. So much goes on before we get to the Kabbalah tree, infinities of supernal infinities. So much goes on before we get to Bion's grid and O-grams. Unknown sub-domains giving rise to emergent states and capacities. What we call the Jungian or Freudian unconscious are not beginning points but results of unnameable processes we try to imagine but cannot truly conceive. Infinites beyond imagining.

We might call the O-grams or grid a kind of tree. Bion calls the former "a pictorial schematic formulation". He is wary of directional, causal type formulations and prefers multi-directional complexity. Trees grow from bottom up but need nourishment from above and once the network expands, directionality becomes complicated.

While Bion uses "hierarchical" terms and images, there is a "non-hierarchical" feel as well. Not only does he manage to stretch the vertical horizontally. I think of Deleuze and Guattari (1987) on the rhizome as model, growing every which way, all kinds of under-ground possibilities, not defined vertically. Bion likes to wonder what experience is like from the vertex of digestion, respiration, proprio-ception, kinaesthesia—not confined to a backbone or arboreal model. He substitutes the term "vertex" for "point of view" so as to minimise visual dominance. Deleuze likes to emphasise that with the rhizome every point is connected with every other point (which is also the case with the Kabbalah tree and Bion's function, states, and capacity charts). The rhizome more easily illustrates a sense of no beginning or end, always in process, in the middle, no "centre" or "one" (not the religious one-and-many). This comes closer to Bion's feel of complex processes creating themselves as they go along or in the gestalt psychology phrase, the spontaneous self-creation of processes. My feeling is that Bion is not bound to any one model, using field and quantum physics notions as well as models drawn from history, reli-gion, philosophy, mathematics, biology, art—almost anything that touches him. In one of his last seminars, in spite of, or in addition to, earlier discussions of science, he spoke of psychoanalysis as art, emotions as colours on the palette (Bion, 1978).

One thing I never much liked in religions is emphasis on "right-eousness". The victory of the righteous, the good ones. Emphasis on the righteous makes me feel like a failure. From this point of view, I *am* a failure. How good can you be? Bible characters are pretty mixed. Even the righteous were pretty flawed. I have never felt myself among the righteous. I would not say I'm totally "wrong", but I'm not "right". I have written about a sense of "something wrong" in several places (1999, 2009). One thing I have not cared for in Rabbi Shimon or Rabbi Nachman stories is their emphasis on a higher place in heaven, a room closer to God. Maybe it is just a way of speaking—for example, someone says or does something especially good and Rabbi Shimon congratulates him on having a higher place in the world to come. Something about this does not fit my personality. First of all, I was always slouchy, never upright. I began doing gym work in my seventies with a couple of trainers who always wanted to make my body do things it didn't want to do. My body has found ways of compensating for psychic pain, its own wisdom or dumbness, but it works well enough overall. I learned the hard way that you have to be careful forcing it this or that way as it can get injured. You have to respect its "solutions" or adaptations, even if you wish they were better. I picture an old tree gnarled and knotted growing around trauma points. A body deals with so much trauma and finds its own knotted ways to survive. Nevertheless, I benefited enormously from various forms of body work, starting with bioenergetics in my twenties. I felt it opened rather than injured, taking into account depths of blockages and working with and through them, as if it worked inside them. I think of a Taoist saying, "In a storm, the reed bends and the oak breaks".

Our upright body follows an arboreal model, as do the *sephirot* and *chakras* (the latter with the variation of sitting upright rather than standing). Yet, we can lie down, live horizontally, which most trees cannot do. In this we share something with the rhizome. There are ways that what it does outwardly, we do inwardly, aspects of psyche–mind (thoughts, feelings, sensations) intertwining, growing in haphazard, unpredictable directions, all parts feeding each other. To some extent, this is true of trees, too. I have always been fascinated that a tree can be alive and dead at the same time. Applying this to myself has been helpful: I do not have to be just one thing, all alive or dead. I can be more alive in some ways, and on the dead side in others. There are many ways to be alive and dead. To some extent, we have to deaden aspects of aliveness to survive. Deadening mechanisms in response to trauma are important. Of course, they can go too far and we feel too dead, too long. In such a state, for some, even a little advent of aliveness is threatening.

Bion writes of how threatening aliveness can be and how deadness can be almost soothing, if it were not so painful. Yet, people get boxed into living with the pain of deadness rather than opening to still greater fears.

* * *

Yet, there is also freedom in self-nullification, beyond depression and defensive deadness. Earlier, I talked about states of struggle and grace, a need to repair and unify as well as tear apart. Kabbalah–Chassidus also places a good deal on developing a capacity to nullify oneself, to become nothing. A morning prayer upon waking awakens awareness that God creates us and everything from nothing every day. You feel different nuances of nothing in the background of your being, for example, the nothing you were for all the aeons before you were born. Many children puzzle about the time they were not, the vast nothing through eternities of time before birth and after death. From nothing to nothing, interlaced with nothing. Yet, you are something, someone.

To translate this psychologically, we have a double capacity to be nothing and something. We can take a vacation from being someone, from having to maintain an identity. We can dive into nothingness, shed imprisoning skins of personality, our personal bars, feel free of ourselves for a time. I represent this by using Bion's bi-conditional sign, a double arrow between Hebrew words for nothing (*ayin*) and being (*yesh*): *ayin* ↔ *yesh*. Double–directional flow. Now I am nothing, now something, now both in varying ways and combinations. In this mode of experience, nothing-and-being are not separate. Both are ways we feel.

There is some similarity here to Rabbi Shimon's vision at the end: separate and not separate, one with God yet at one with oneself. A distinction–union experience. Separate-and-one. Both together, a paradoxical structure of experience (Eigen, 2011, Chapters One and Two). There are many variations.

Suppose a moment of almost total nullification, as if not only oneself but all existence is nullified. In the scenario I am sketching, we do not know when we begin, when anything begins. Suppose at some point a feeling of mysterious presence begins to form. The Untouchable touches us and from nothing comes something. All existence comes into being with us, we with it. At some point, we rush into life, explore, use ourselves and others, but a memory of nothing remains in the background. There might come a time when we search for this capacity, a time we need it to clear ourselves out, get rid of some of the noise that threatens to deafen something precious. Something further opens. We move from our noisy self to our null self, a null dimension. A place to start over, fresh, repeatedly. It might sound odd, but we begin to have opportunity to cultivate null dimensions, capacity to be nothing; to cultivate both being and not being as a path of growth. A double capacity that needs care and enrichment, part of the garden we are given to cultivate.

*   *   *

Nothing as envisioned in Kabbalah can get very complicated. Nothing has many layers and dimensions and infinities, filled with possibilities. Sometimes it is called "what" or "not". When you contact it in meditation, it can be awesome—even the unfolding of infinite moments of peace can be awesome. At other times, there are delicate soul shivers. There are mysterious layers of nothing and dimensions that can have no name or conceiving, beyond the dichotomy nothing–being, mystery beyond mystery. Chassidus envisions soul created from nothing, filled with nothing, going back to nothing—all the time. The space opened by self-nullification is "filled" by God.

Bion, too, questions beginnings and endings. When he speaks about terminal cancer, he wonders, what can termination mean? Termination of what? He emphasises the importance of working with what *can* be worked with, undeterred by a terminal prognosis. If a person is still alive and you are working with him or her, focus on what is possible between you in the time you have. In face of a terminal prognosis, worlds *can* open that were closed before. A therapist can help mediate and support this opening.

One great example of profound self-nullifcation is the *Shechinah*, God's feminine Presence. In the *Zohar*, *Shechinah* has no light of her own. She is more like the moon, reflecting the sun's light. I interpret this to refer to that part of us that reflects the light of others. As a therapist, you have capacity to reflect the light of others, the light coming to you. Kohut (1971) describes aspects of this capacity as empathically mirroring states and needs of others. Sometimes, I feel the word "mirror" is too material, too hard and fast. The responsive feeling represented by *Shechinah* has no shape or form.

To be a being that reflects the light of others as well as having one's own light, one's own spark. One's own light can be self-affirming and be a reflector. If your light is turned on maximally all the time, there might be little room for the light of others. If your light can adapt to changing circumstances, the light of others can be seen in yours. And sometimes, you have to turn your light off to let a light of another shine and be experienced. In that moment of nullification, you free yourself. Nullification allows a moment free of self-persecutory demands. You should be this, you should do that, you should be the centre of attention—a moment free of this nagging, free of the tyranny of self. Not bye-bye self forever, but some degrees of freedom.

While Chassidus asserts that we have a share in the way the Unknowable works through its emanations, creations, formations, and actions, as a secular psychologist I tend to see God mirroring our human capacities. Aspects of our concept of God mirror more and less recognised capacities. More recognised capacities expressed by the *sephirot*, less recognised capacities expressed by unknown infinities beyond them. Perhaps a conception of God as mirroring human capacities suggests a sense that God, too, undergoes self-nullification. And in certain sublime moments, contact is made between our self-nullification and God's.

* * *

One mysterious point in psychoanalysis is Freud's idea of a dream navel, "the spot where it [the dream] reaches down into the un-known" (Freud, 1900a, p. 525). Freud likens it to a mycelium, a fungus, a cousin to Deleuze's fungal rhizome. Tangles of dream thoughts vanishing from sight, popping up as threads of growth any place the fungus extends. A particular vision I have is the vanishing mycelium making its way towards Bion's O. Or just the opposite, emanations of O making their way towards dream life.

* * *

In Bion's O-grams, O is mysteriously situated beneath Root (O-gram 1) and beneath Godhead and Analogues (O-gram 2, p. 10). O as start-ing point, unknown origin. We might picture it as a seed, or perhaps the *Zohar's* "spark of impenetrable darkness" (Matt, 2004, Volume 1, p. 107), a radiant point containing all light, igniting creation. At the same time, O may have no beginning or ending, although we speak of birth and death, realities for us. We swim in seas of images to express what cannot be known, using terms that touch meaningful aspects of our lives.

If you stay with O, you will never see a person exactly the same way. If you stay with O, you will be less likely to box people up. When in New York, Bion said, "If you think you're seeing the same patient, you're seeing the wrong patient". He also spoke of a patient saying, after twelve years of analysis, "I'm just the same as when I started. Nothing has happened here." Bion responded, "Do you mind telling me how you did that?" He went on to say that learning how to stop change would be quite a scientific achievement.

Can one say, by implication, if you are seeing the same O, you are seeing the wrong O? If O is unknowable, we are speaking in figures of speech. If one feels and says, "Everything is the same, nothing has changed", one expresses a real state, a significant experience or way of experiencing, even if this is not possible in reality. On the other hand, if one catches on—deeply catches on—that things are in some ways changing, that transformational processes are always at work, for better or worse, one has more of a chance of experiencing areas of freedom or possible exploration in addition to a sense of the same. One can, to a certain extent, transcend one's current situation or, better, dive into it, be with it, work with it.

Doubleness, as usual, appears. Things are always changing. Things are always the same. Both sentiments expressed as states of being. Perhaps, too, one can learn to hold this doubleness and let it work on you, take you to new mixtures of familiar–unfamiliar places.

*   *   *

O as undetermined "beginning", vanishing like the dream navel from view. Expressing itself as Root with emergent capacities (O-gram 1, p. 10). In some phenomenological sense, everything grows from this root feeling, this root sensation, although we may intuit, posit, sense intimations of O giving rise to Root.

Different root sensations for different people or the same person at different times. A root sense from which things grow. At the same time, Bion tells us we could begin with any part of the O-gram, any emergent capacity or state that marks one's life, and find one's way to others. Although O is at the bottom, we can begin with the top, Music, Religion, Sculpture, Poetry, or Painting, and find one's way to O.

One could begin with any *chakra* and animate the others. Start with the crown and the downflow will lead to the base; start with the base and the upflow will lead to the crown. I was told to visualise a serpent coiled at the base, rising up the spine through various stations as you progress in psycho-spiritual freedom. But where is the base of the spine? Where does it start? Where does it go? The perineum, between anus and genitals? I have had teachers say, "Breathe with your asshole." The base is very deep in the body.

The *sephira, Malchut,* is associated with feet. Beyond the seven *chakras* usually emphasised, there are many *chakras* in the feet and a variety of ways to access them. One can, for example, activate them or become more aware of their activation through meditation or massage. Not just foot massage, but cranial massage. Cranial therapy can reach the feet and footwork can reach the cranium. As with the *sephirot,* one can begin with any *chakra* and reach others in interlaced openness. There are many *chakras* outside the usual count and my sense is there are many psychophysical capacities with reverberations beyond the standardised *sephirot* stations. Much interweaving beyond the vertical (Eigen, 1986).

*   *   *

The *sephirot* and *chakras* have physical, psychological, and spiritual dimensions. The *sephirot* graph aspects of the body from top to bottom or bottom to top. We schematised this with *Chochma* (wisdom), *Binah* (understanding), *Daat* (knowledge) as the head. *Chesed* (mercy, loving kindness) and *Gevurah* (strength, judgement) as the right and left arms. *Tiferet* (Beauty) as heart. *Netzach* (endurance, persistence) and *Hod* (flexibility, openness) as the hips and legs. *Yesod* (fecundity) as genitals. *Malchut* (kingdom, *Shechinah*) as feet. On a purely physical plane, when you are dancing or running or moving your hips back and forth, you might feel moments of special hip-strength and fluidity and tingle all over. A tingling that all the *chakras/sephirot* reverberate to. A tingling that is physical but not just physical as it spreads through many capacities and areas and opens a sense of the ineffable. As I have often said (2006a), sensation is, or can be, ineffable. Sensation can lead you to divinity, God sensation spreading all through you.

*   *   *

I mentioned that *chakras* and *sephirot* can be located through sensory and muscular sensations all through your being. Let us not be too dogmatic about this fluidity. You can feel the divine feeling all through your being, in your cells, your pores. The Zen master's one finger Zen—moving one finger upward—can feel so good. Every movement can be blissful.

The root feeling can be anywhere for you. It could be in any of the *sephirot* or *chakras*, depending on where you are located at the moment. Often the *hara*, just below your navel, is emphasised. I like all the spots, but my special spot for most of my life—not as special now as other spots have caught up with it—is *Tiferet*, the heart *chakra* or nearby. There [pointing to my chest] is an area I call the infinitesimal infinity point. It tells me to go this way or that way, softer, louder, yes, no, stop, go. It seems to be a source of values. The *Upanishads* speaks of a point of self no bigger than a thumbnail. For Bion and Kabbalah, the point is even smaller.

For the moment, let me speak of a sigma point. Bion uses the letter sigma for Teilhard de Chardin's (2008) noosphere. De Chardin writes of a biosphere (living being), psychosphere (psychological existence), and noosphere (spiritual being), an evolution of emergent capacities. As a child, he was in love with rocks and he became a palaeontologist. Rocks were alive for him. Perhaps he saw God in rocks (Eigen, 2007, Chapter One). He grew up not only to be a palaeontologist, but also a Jesuit priest. He felt the noosphere was evolving into a greater unity that would some day unite humankind spiritually, perhaps a kind of universal interpenetration of spirit.

Bion wanted to avoid usage of the term "sphere". He wanted to keep the reality pointed to open, not prematurely saturated with particular images. This is something like his substituting the term vertex for point of view, an attempt to avoid a visual bias. Bion felt that as infants everything seems animate, and that as we grow we learn to differentiate inanimate from animate. We learn to deaden experience to function in "reality". I suspect for Bion reality *is* alive.

It is rich to contemplate de Chardin's childhood rocks as animated, as he must have experienced them. And reverie how for him this animate sense grew in dimensionality. Bion referred to de Chardin late in life (1994b, p. 313). Bion spoke of a need to keep on evolving lest we kill ourselves off and a better creature take our place. Evolving not only in capacities but in being able to learn to use our capacities. He appreciated de Chardin's depiction of further evolution of a spiritual dimension that would bring us all together in ways we cannot conceive now. A number of times, towards the end of his life, Bion questioned the idea of ending, and de Chardin's depiction of a noosphere appealed to Bion's sense of further dimensions as yet unknown.

*   *   *

We just cannot stop here. More has to happen, further layers of organisation. *Ein Sof* and O can be seen, in part, as giving rise to emergent capacities. If, sometimes, we equate them with chaos or nothingness, perhaps we are hinting at potential for happening, from nothing to *yesh*, the 10,000 things, the bells and whistles of life. A perpetually embryonic element through which always more is possible.

Bion and Winnicott often write of precocious or premature organisation of a potential growth process. For example, an inchoate emotional pressure being shaped into form too quickly, missing the unfolding of feeling. Even a dream narrative might give premature form to vague emotional pressures, slanting them in one or another direction and leaving other elements out. A kind of premature ejaculation of unknown feeling into a narrative or concept. At the same time, the dream narrative and imagery could give hints of emotional realities squeezed into dream form.

In a way, you can look at Bion's grid as successive organisations of emotional experience that is dimly felt and known. With each step along the grid, the embryonic emotion is further shaped and defined, lessening the original impact and losing other possible contours. One might dramatise this by saying the feelings we have are ours at the expense of aspects of feelings left behind, aborted. That is one reason Bion urges us to return to more fragmented states, start from scratch, and lessen the hold of built up narrative organisations of emotion that remains largely unfelt and unmet.

He feels most of the session takes place, or should take place, on row C, dream thoughts, dreams, myths, rather than a more conceptual plane. At least, then, we have somewhat more of a chance to taste a bit of the feeling seeking birth, even if it is prematurely ushered into image–narrative form, gaining something, losing a lot. So much of what we experience are bits wrested out of larger unknown contexts. That Bion includes dream thoughts hints of Freud's dream navel, which brings us to the brink of the unknown, the vanishing point of the dream, the point that disappears into a larger, unperceived emotional sea.

*   *   *

There was a time when psychoanalysis advocated creative regression. One drops into a less organised state, temporarily shedding built up skins of personality, so that one has a taste of starting fresh. Winnicott (1992; Eigen, 2004) wrote of dropping into a primordial madness then spontaneously coming back, the better for it. Balint (1967) wrote of re-tasting early harmonious interweaving or mix-up, in hope of offsetting or correcting a sense of basic fault in personality. Using a bit of Kabbalah and Bion, I would like to add a felt moment of vanishing into O emanating us, a double movement in one. Or returning to God re-creating us in divine embrace.

*   *   *

Well, I didn't realise we had reached our vanishing point. We have run out of time. Perhaps I can stretch a few seconds and make a few more remarks and take some questions. The grid tells us concepts have a long history, that what we call emotions have a long journey from an unknown background through successive forming processes. Unknown background pressures reach through beta and alpha elements to dreams and myths and the growth of concepts. We learn to think about feeling. Each step of the way, more of the feeling is lost as some part of it is caught and refined. By implication, Bion is reminding us to be cautious about what we think we know. We may think we know a lot about ourselves, but the emotions we can focus on are a small part of where they came from.

We might find something in a formula modified from Ricoeur (1986): affect gives rise to image gives rise to thought. I would like to speak for a felt sense, a kind of root sense that plays a role in all the things you come up with. You keep returning to a felt sense and see what more comes. Often, when I write about therapy, I try to contact a basic felt sense of the session and let that speak. Keep returning to a basic felt sense, which itself can undergo development and lead to another felt sense.

If one looks at O-gram 1 (p. 10), one sees God as a "form" (perhaps in a Platonic sense) that developed from a more primordial felt sense, Root or O, the O of God.

Back to the felt sense. Let the felt sense create. Maybe new eternals or aspects of psyches will appear. They *have* to.

One quick note on O-gram 2 (p. 10). In this O-gram, we see arrows pointing downward. There is much to say, but here only a little.

Arrows point down from alpha to beta and from beta to O. You would think the opposite. You would expect everything to grow from O, arrows pointing upward. Recall that any part of an O-gram can lead to any other, as every *sephira* and *chakra* can lead to every other. Processes are multi-directional and we select ways to work with them.

One special meaning of the downward arrows fits in with Bion's emphasis on the importance of conscious becoming unconscious, seemingly opposite to Freud's dictum, where id is ego will be (I will be where it is). A lot of our life is unlived, partly because of limitations of our makeup. One function of therapy is to help people let more of their lives in. Support growth of psyche so that it can tolerate more living. To let the reality of what we encounter in, so that it becomes part of us, part of deeper levels of our being that support conscious awareness. To let more of ourselves in, a deeper sense of ourselves. A deeper sense that flows from and needs support of unconscious life. Support that saves us from being stranded from ourselves in upper stories, what Merleau-Ponty calls high-altitude thinking.

We might learn a skill like karate or Tai Chi step by step with hard work of conscious practice. But for it to truly become part of us, it must seep into deeper levels of being, more primary strata. It becomes part of our felt sense of movement, like a musician's felt sense, available for new intuitive flow. It must become part of the O of our beings.

*   *   *

Before we are asked to leave, does anyone want to ask something?

Comment: I just want to thank you. I feel lit up.

Response: Are you fired up? (Laughter).

Question: When will the next seminar be?

Response: I hope in about half a year. On interfaces of Kabbalah and psychoanalysis—on souls, states, worlds, capacities. But, you know, I am not vanishing into a cave until then. I give a seminar Tuesday afternoons at my office. You are all welcome to attend.

Questioner: OK, thank you so much, thanks.

Question: Could we have the next seminar start off where you left off now?

Response: First of all, at my age, I'd just like to be here for the next one. Thank you, though, for wanting more. We can pick up wherever O picks us up. Let's keep on O'ing.

REFERENCES

Arendt, H. (1970). *On Violence*. New York: Houghton Mifflin Harcourt.

Arendt, H. (2006). *On Revolution*. New York: Penguin Classics.

Arnheim, R. (1969). *Visual Thinking*. Berkeley, CA: University of California Press.

Balint, M. (1967). *The Basic Fault*. London: Routledge.

Berdyaev, N. (1958). *Dostoevsky*. New York: Meridian.

Bion, W. R. (1970). *Attention and Interpretation*. London: Karnac, 1984.

Bion, W. R. (1978). *A Seminar Held in Paris in 1978*. www.psychoanalysis.org.uk/bion78.htm

Bion, W. R. (1990). *A Memoir of the Future*. London: Karnac.

Bion, W. R. (1994a). *Clinical Seminars and Other Works*, F. Bion (Ed.). London: Karnac.

Bion, W. R. (1994b). *Cogitations*, F. Bion (Ed.). London: Karnac.

Blomfield, V. (2011). *Gautama Buddha: The Life and Teachings of the Awakened One*. London: Quercus.

Bohm, D. (1996). *Wholeness and the Implicate Order*. London: Routledge.

De Chardin, P. (2008). *The Phenomenon of Man*. New York: HarperCollins.

Deleuze, G., & Guattari, F. (1987). *A Thousand Plateaus: Capitalism and Schizophrenia*, B. Massumi (Trans.). Minneapolis, MN: University of Minnesota Press.

Eigen, M. (1973). Abstinence and the schizoid ego. *International Journal of Psychoanalysis, 54*: 493–497. Reprinted in: *The Electrified Tightrope* (2004).

Eigen, M. (1981). The area of faith in Winnicott, Lacan and Bion. *International Journal of Psychoanalysis, 62*: 413–433. Reprinted in: *The Electrified Tightrope*, 2004.

Eigen, M. (1986). *The Psychotic Core*. London: Karnac, 2004.

Eigen, M. (1993). *The Electrified Tightrope*. A. Phillips (Ed.). London: Karnac, 2004.

Eigen, M. (1996). *Psychic Deadness*. London: Karnac, 2004.

Eigen, M. (1998). *The Psychoanalytic Mystic*. London: Free Association Books.

Eigen, M. (1999). *Toxic Nourishment*. London: Karnac.

Eigen, M. (2001). *Damaged Bonds*. London: Karnac.

Eigen, M. (2002). *Rage*. Middletown, CT: Wesleyan University Press.

Eigen, M. (2004). *The Sensitive Self*. Middletown, CT: Wesleyan University Press.

Eigen, M. (2005). *Emotional Storm*. Middletown, CT: Wesleyan University Press.

Eigen, M. (2006a). *Lust*. Middletown, CT: Wesleyan University Press.

Eigen, M. (2006b). *Age of Psychopathy*. www.psychoanalysis-and-therapy. com/human_nature/eigen/pref.html

Eigen, M. (2007). *Feeling Matters*. London: Karnac.

Eigen, M. (2009). *Flames From the Unconscious: Trauma, Madness and Faith*. London: Karnac.

Eigen, M. (2011). *Contact With the Depths*. London: Karnac.

Eigen, M. (2012a). *Kabbalah and Psychoanalysis*. London: Karnac.

Eigen, M. (2012b). On Winnicott's clinical innovations in the analysis of adults. *International Journal of Psychoanalysis, 93*: 1449-1459.

Eigen, M. (2013). Response by Michael Eigen: We never recover from being human. *International Journal of Psychoanalysis, 94*: 118–121.

Einstein, A. (1950). Letter written in 1950, quoted in *The New York Times*, 29 March, 1972. For another version of this letter and an explanation, A. Calaprice (Ed.), *The New Quotable Einstein*. Princeton University Press, 2005.

Freud, S. (1900a). *The Interpretation of Dreams*. S.E., 5. London: Hogarth.

Freud, S. (1911c). *Psycho-analytic Notes on an Autobiographical Account of a Case of Paranoia*. S.E., 12: 3–82. London: Hogarth.

Green, A. (1975). The analyst, symbolization and absence in the analytic setting (on changes in analytic practice and analytic experience). *International Journal of Psychoanalysis, 56*: 1–22.

Khan, M. (1996). *The Privacy of the Self*. London: Karnac.

Klein, M. (1945). Notes on some schizoid mechanisms. In: M. Klein, P. Heimann, S. Isaacs, & J. Riviere (Eds.), *Developments in Psychoanalysis* (pp. 292–320). London: Hogarth Press (1952).

Kohut, H. (1971). *The Analysis of the Self*. Chicago, IL: University of Chicago Press, 2009.

Levinas, E. (1999). *Alterity and Transcendence*, M. B. Smith (Trans.). New York: Columbia University Press.

Liebes, Y. (1993). *Studies in the Zohar*. Albany, NY: State University of New York.

Mathers, S. L. M. (1887). *The Kabbalah Unveiled*. Whitefish, Montana: Kessinger.

Matt, D. C. (1998). *God and the Big Bang: Discovering Harmony between Science and Spirituality*. Woodstock, VT: Jewish Lights.

Matt, D. C. (2002). *Zohar: Annotated and Explained*. Woodstock, VT: SkyLight Paths.

Matt, D. C. (2004). *The Zohar*, D. C. Matt (Trans.), Pritzger Edition. Stanford, CA: Stanford University Press.

Matte-Blanco, I. (1975). *The Unconscious as Infinite Sets: An Essay in Bi-logic*. London: Karnac, 1980.

Matte-Blanco, I. (1988). *Thinking, Feeling and Being*. London: Routledge.

Meltzer, D. (2008). *Sexual States of Mind*. London: Harris Meltzer Trust.

Milner, M. (1987). *The Suppressed Madness of Sane Men: Forty-Four Years of Exploring Psychoanalysis*. London: Routledge.

Molofsky, M. (2009). Some thoughts on synthesizing core concepts of the chakra system, Jewish mystical tradition and Qi Gong. Accessed at: http.//merlemolofsky.com/sample-writings.html.

Ricoeur, P. (1986). *The Symbolism of Evil*. Boston, MA: Beacon Press.

Roustang, F. (1980). *Psychoanalysis Never Lets Go*, N. Lukacher (Trans.). Baltimore, MD: Johns Hopkins University Press.

Schneerson, M. M. (1978). *On the Essence of Chassidus*, Y. Greenberg & S. S. Handelman (Trans.). Brooklyn, NY: Kehot Publication Society.

Tanahashi, K. (Ed.) (1995). *Moon in a Dewdrop: Writings of Zen Master Dogen*. New York: North Point Press.

Winnicott, D. W. (1988). *Human Nature*. London: Free Association Books.

Winnicott, D. W. (1992). *Psychoanalytic Explorations*, C. Winnicott, R. Shepherd, & M. Davis (Eds.). Cambridge, MA: Harvard University Press.

Zahavy, Z. (1977). *Idra Zuta Kadisha: The Lesser Holy Assembly*. New York: Sage.

Zalman, S. (1797). *Likutei Amarim (Tanya)*. Brooklyn, NY: Kehot Publication Society, 1996.

INDEX

For Product Safety Concerns and Information please contact our EU
representative GPSR@taylorandfrancis.com
Taylor & Francis Verlag GmbH, Kaufingerstraße 24, 80331 München, Germany